AUSTRIA

I SCHÖNBRUNN

AUSTRIA

SACHEVERELL SITWELL

TONI SCHNEIDERS

194 PHOTOGRAVURE PLATES

7 PLATES IN COLOUR

A STUDIO BOOK

THE VIKING PRESS · NEW YORK

DR JOHNSON, who was never permitted this indulgence in his own person, said that the grand object of travel was to see the shores of the Mediterranean. In their place he had to content himself with the waters of the Outer Hebrides. No doubt he had in mind the classical sites along the golden littoral from Tarragona to the temples of Paestum, and down to Sicily, and was embracing in one fine phrase the Tiber and the shores of Greece.

All of which we say because in this beautiful book of photographs of different parts of Austria there is the persistent shadow of the Holy Roman Empire. This may seem shadowy enough to Englishmen who have been told the silly phrase that the Empire in question was 'neither Holy, nor Roman, nor even an Empire', but it was real enough to those many millions of persons who lived in it. Neither is it of recent demise, nor of distant date. Francis II, the last 'Roman' Emperor, began reigning in 1792 and resigned the title becoming Emperor of Austria instead in 1806, in order it may have been to forestall Napoleon who was fresh from victory at Austerlitz. He died in 1835, while Metternich his prime minister lived until 1859. The vast dominions of the Habsburgs had come to them, not through war but by inheritance through marriage, and we could conclude this too rapid summary of what was for centuries a huge historical entity with the remark that the great men of this unique conglomeration of races with its heart and mind in Vienna were not painters, nor poets, but musicians—Haydn, Mozart, Beethoven, Schubert, Brahms (by adoption), Johann Strauss, Lehar (if you like), Bruckner, Mahler. To show that Austria has, as well, lovely scenery of every description and buildings by great architects is the purpose of this present volume.

There are many ways of arriving in Austria, but for myself I can think of none better than that moment of looking up at the huge wings and twin towers of Melk across the Danube waters, perhaps spending the night at Dürnstein, and knowing you are to arrive on the morrow at Vienna. Others may prefer coming to it from the snows of Kitzbühel or St Anton, after a music festival at Salzburg, or by Alpine pass from Italy, but it is in Vienna that we find ourselves, inevitably. For here are so many different kinds of self-expression in the form of sight-seeing. There are those who will want to go immediately to see the Brueghels in the picture gallery; or the Coronation robes and regalia of the Holy Roman Emperors in the Schatz-kammer; or the white Lippizaner horses in the Spanish Riding School; and at night drink Grinzinger or Gumpoldskirchener in a wine cellar and perhaps listen to a Hungarian band. For myself, where Vienna is concerned, I have two regrets which share a little in common with each other; never to have seen a performance by the Lippizaner horses and to have missed by only a few years a sight of the Hungarian Life Guard. They were quartered (until November, 1918) in the palace built by Fischer von Erlach for Prince Trautson; they wore a scarlet Hussar uniform enriched with silver lace, a tiger-skin pellisse hanging from the shoulder, boots of yellow leather, and a high fur cap surmounted by a heron's plume, while their grey horses had green housings and silver bridles. This 'corps d'élite of Europe' was founded by Maria-Theresa and their colonel became, on appointment, a Baron of the Holy Roman Empire. It has been said that it was the sound of the high trumpets of their mounted band playing the Rákóczy March as they rode along the streets that made Sibelius, then a student in Vienna, become deter-mined in his mind to be a composer. But, to continue . . .

The white Lippizaner horses, of noble Arabian, Neapolitan and Spanish blood are born jet-black, and only become milk-white of skin when two or three years old. Their equestrian ballets are a living relic of the medieval past. And now what I wrote in my opening sentences should be extended into saying that just as the classical past survived and had some sort of con-tinuity into Byzantium of the Eastern Emperors, so the Empire of the West through Charle-magne and his successors had continued representation through the Habsburgs into modern times. Just as the Byzantines had retreated to the Bosphorus, so the medieval Emperors of the West had long left the Mediterranean to reign beyond the Alps. But it could be argued that if you cannot achieve the grand object of travel, which is Italy, in default of Florence or Rome or Venice, you had better go to Vienna, the Habsburg capital. As to the white Lippizaners, they are eloquent of the age of Charles V, a monarch who could be qualified as the greatest man in the sense of inherited or hereditary importance since the time of Charlemagne. It was Charles V who divided the Empire, the Spanish and Italian and Flemish dominions going with the Americas to his son Philip II, and the German domains with the title of Emperor going to his own brother, Ferdinand. Charles is therefore the founder of the Spanish, and Ferdinand the progenitor of the German line of the Habsburgs. Of Charles there is not much evidence in Austria as he spent most of his life in Spain but, at least in Innsbruck, there is no forgetting his grandfather Maximilian, 'the last of the Knights' and patron of Albrecht Dürer.

In Vienna one of the first things we see is the double-headed black eagle of the Habsburgs in

II FORCHTENSTEIN CASTLE

tilework on the roof of St Stephen's. And in a town where so much else is gay and lively it is with some foreboding that we penetrate its Stygian gloom. The Gothic style is not suited to Vienna, a city which in all essentials dates from after the raising of the Turkish siege in 1683. Far more typical of Vienna than St Stephen's is the domed Karlskirche of Fischer von Erlach, though it is perhaps symptomatic of the Habsburgs, too, that the pair of columns standing in front of it in duplication of Trajan's Column should have for subject of their spiral reliefs, not martial scenes but episodes from the life of San Carlo Borromeo. Not that many persons during two centuries and a half can have had the patience to unravel them. This, at least, was Vienna before the age of music, when Gluck was in his first infancy and Haydn not yet born.

To the Hofburg it is impossible not to direct one's steps again and again; whether to the Schatzkammer, to the Redouten-Säle at night in order to listen to Mozart, to the Library, or to the aforesaid Spanish Riding School. The Coronation robes, which are really those of the Norman Kings of Sicily, of Saracen workmanship with inscriptions in Arabic, are wonderful indeed, being the most marvellous existing regalia of their sort and kind. Excessively curious, too, are the gloves and slippers and red silk stockings of the anointed Emperor. There are, as well, the herald's costumes of the Order of the Golden Fleece; and, of another and different world eight centuries later in date, the cradle of the Duc de Reichstadt, or as it reads better in French, *le berceau du Roi de Rome*. Somewhere among these treasures must be the blue and silver embroidered (*blau-silberreiche*) liturgical vestments given by Maria-Theresa to the Hofburg-kapelle, which were among the sensations of the 1958 exhibition of the Age of Rococo in Munich. So we find that all ages and styles are represented in the Schatzkammer.

But we will now start on a quick tour of the Baroque buildings of Vienna, the monuments of her golden age of architecture which preceded by a few years her great age of music. There is no better place to begin this than in the Hofbibliothek, the most splendid library hall imagin-able, in a style of which Sir John Vanbrugh is the English master. Seeing it, one must regret there is no library built by him in Oxford or Cambridge. Instead, there is a library to rival it at the University of Coimbra in Portugal, with three halls opening out of one another which have lacquered galleries and bookshelves in a light green, then a darker, and then a shade like orange Niger leather. But this library in Vienna was prototype for others built in several of the Baroque abbeys in Austria, and we will find that these same abbeys have generally a Kaisersaal as well, a throne room built traditionally for the Kaiser to receive homage in on his way to be crowned at Frankfurt. And now it remains to say that the Karlskirche and the Hofbibliothek, and the Spanish Riding School, as well, are all from the plans of Fischer von Erlach, and all built to the order of Charles VI, father of Maria-Theresa, and last male Habsburg of the Austrian line.

III THE CLOCK TOWER AT GRAZ

The High Baroque of Vienna is also to be seen in splendour in the Summer and Winter Palaces of Prince Eugen of Savoy, his Summer Palace being the beautiful and famous Belvedere. This great soldier was our ally in the Wars of the Spanish Succession, the purpose of which was to put his master Charles VI on the Spanish throne in place of the progeny of Louis XIV, a project which failed though Marlborough and Prince Eugen won all the battles against the French. It has been thought that Prince Eugen may have been, himself, a son of Louis XIV which gives piquancy to the situation. His mother was Olympia Mancini, niece of Cardinal Mazarin, and decidedly a mistress of *le Roi Soleil*.

The name of another architect, Lukas von Hildebrandt, now occurs beside that of Fischer von Erlach because he was employed in both palaces of Prince Eugen. The staircase of the Belvedere is very typical of his manner, though I would say that the stair of the Winter Palace is even cleverer and more remarkable in the handling. It makes an effect of extraordinary grandeur out of an awkward and confined space, perhaps the more so because the architect was proud of his cleverness and makes no attempt to cover up his sleight-of-hand. There will be those who prefer seeking out the narrow old courts of Vienna and the old wine houses so evocative of the time of Schubert and the Biedermeier (a kind of parallel to Balzacian Paris), and those others who look for the palaces, Auersperg, Harrach, Kinsky, Liechtenstein, Schönborn, and Schwarzenberg which echo the old splendours of the monarchy and its noble families with great estates in Bohemia and Hungary. And of course there are the high horn-beam hedges of Schönbrunn, though I have to admit to being disappointed by the interior of the Palace. Of the far-famed 'Spanish' formality and etiquette of the Habsburg court there is little sign at Schönbrunn, but the scene of that will have been the Hofburg. How much the present writer, at least, would wish to have seen one of the court processions, that on Corpus Christi for instance, when the Kaiser and the Archdukes rode in golden coaches drawn by six and eight white horses, surrounded by the Hungarian, Italian and Galician Guard and the Trabants (who were halberdiers)!

But music is of inseparable association with Vienna and, as well, the shades of Mayerling. The Crown Prince Rudolf in the rôle of Hamlet still haunts the place, and what was in reality little more than a sordid tragedy darkens the scene and taints the ending of last century. It is perhaps impossible to exaggerate the degree to which the Viennese population must have been permeated with music at this time after a hundred years and more of great musicians living in their midst—even before the coming of radio and gramophone—reaching to its most far-fetched expression in the *Fiaker-Walzer* (cabmen's waltzes) that form a little world to themselves of intrigue and gaiety, for cabdrivers were to the contemporaries of Johann Strauss what gondoliers were to Venetians of the eighteenth century, that is to say, they carried messages, they were

IV ADMONT MONASTERY, THE LIBRARY

in a privileged position as onlookers of life, and they knew a lot of other peoples' secrets. During the latter part of the century Vienna may have been the most delightful of all towns to live in, and withal the capital city of a great Empire, though after ordering a meal in an outdoor restaurant in some Austrian town one may wonder how efficiently that empire was run as the hours slip by in waiting for *Forellen* while sitting underneath the trees. But part of the fascination of the Old Austria must have been the remote nature of its provinces and the mixture of races: Moravia, Hungary, Bukovina, the Banat, Bosnia, Dalmatia, Galicia, Transylvania, Slovenia, Croatia, all looking to Vienna as their capital.

And into one of the few remaining of these distant areas we now advance, leaving Vienna for the Burgenland. Not that it is remote as the miles go, for it is less than sixty miles away. But it is a flat and marshy plain unlike any other part of Austria, and indeed quite Hungarian in character, or reminiscent, at any rate, of the flat part of Hungary, which is the more obvious when we know that a great portion of the Esterházy properties were in the Burgenland, and that Liszt was born near here at Raiding. In fact, we are bound for Eisenstadt, one of the two main châteaux of the Esterházys, Eszterháza their other castle being over the Hungarian frontier. Eisenstadt is a big, deserted-looking palace with all the gloom of such structures when their glory has departed. One wonders if it was any less depressing during the years when Hadyn conducted his own music here, for the comfort and splendour of such palaces can become exaggerated. Forchtenstein, an old castle which contained the treasures of the family, including the family jacket of pearls and the diamond waistcoat worn at the coronation of George IV, is nearby and was guarded of old by 'a small garrison of invalids from the Prince's grenadiers'. Those days are over, if to no one's decided benefit; as, indeed, are those, not only of a composer like Haydn fitted in youth with a musical grammar in set forms which enabled him to write, with all his other music, eighty string quartets and more than a hundred symphonies, but also of a virtuoso and pyrotechnician of Liszt's nature. No one of them, or their like, Haydn, Liszt, or Esterházy, to apostrophize a whole family as one person, will be born again.

The great abbeys of Austria now come into sight, beginning with Stift Altenburg, which is near Krems in Lower Austria, so that we have to come to it from the Burgenland, backwards, from behind Vienna, having already seen that city. This Benedictine abbey is one of the most interesting places in the whole country. The church of Altenburg has a great fresco'd dome by Paul Troger, which as a feat of execution and imagination is altogether exceptional and superior to anything of the date in Italy. But it is above all the Library and the crypt under that which are remarkable, for the first has at its central axis two great detached piers with prancing horses and another pair with sphinxes, and the painted marble is of a combination of colours, porphyry red and milky blue, which raise the painting of *scagliola* into an art on its own, while the crypt has

V VOLDERS

frescoes from an unknown hand of the Dance of Death, a great series of fantasias with skeletons as actors. These, at least, are unique and there is nothing like them. A little of their quality of wild and grotesque fancy can be gathered from the illustration, which gives a general idea of them but does not show the detail.

The abbeys now continue in earnest as we go up the Danube. Göttweig, which is a splendid fragment—though on its hilltop it looks anything but that from below—has a fine staircase and a ceiling frescoe by Paul Troger. Perhaps Göttweig is hardly worth the long climb to get to it. What is very worthwhile is Dürnstein, one of the most charming of little towns to stay the night in, alive, in warmer months at least, with voices singing and the twanging of the zither, and where in typical Austrian fashion any young woman of the party may be handed a note expressing admiration, and signed 'Papageno'. The tradition of serenades at Dürnstein may be dated back, in fancy, to 1193 when Richard Cœur de Lion was discovered here in prison by his minstrel Blondin, who sang his favourite song to him. There is a charming church here, too, and even a little monastic theatre where Passion plays were given. Dürnstein on the Danube stays a longer time on the memory than many another town.

But now we find Melk rising before us, not in the least resembling Blenheim but on the Blenheim scale. The church interior in dull reds and gold has delightful latticed opera boxes— they are nothing less than that—for the choir, and there is a fine and splendid library in blue and gold with Paul Troger at work, once more, upon the ceiling. The architect in the main responsible for Melk was Jakob Prandtauer, and it could be said in conclusion that even the Post House in the town below is a little building in Baroque style. Those persons who are out of sympathy with the period had better avoid this part of Austria where the great abbeys are situate. Personally, I prefer St Florian to Melk, in part because of its beautiful surrounding of cornlands and cherry or apricot orchards. But the monastery at St Florian is more interesting than the church. It has an open staircase hall in two storeys with openings, two pairs of the apertures being ornamented with great scrolls, while the snow-white double staircase itself has beautiful wrought-iron gates on every landing. Above is a Kaisersaal *à la Bibiena*, and a series of state rooms with tapestries and china stoves, all on the scale to house the Kaiser on his way to Frankfurt to be crowned.

There is another trio of abbeys in this part of Austria, and then the roll is called and their task is done. First is Kremsmünster, always connected in my mind with a ridiculous personal memory because I once asked the concierge in the hotel at Salzburg, but no doubt he was a German and not an Austrian, how much a taxi would cost to go to Kremsmünster, and after an hour's calculation he came back with the fare precisely worked out all the way from Salzburg to Westminster Abbey! At Kremsmünster there is a feature to be seen nowhere else in these

14

monastic arcadias, in the form of five arcaded fish-ponds with fountain statues, and stags' heads lining the whitewashed walls; and there is, also, a splendid Kaisersaal. The Treasury contains the Tassilo Chalice, a church vessel of the eighth century given by Duke Tassilo II of Bavaria, 'that rival of Charlemagne', and founder of the Abbey. A feature of Kremsmünster is a statue of Tassilo as a bearded giant, of Baroque date but in the Wagnerian canon.

Seitenstetten, in beautiful low, green meadows is an abbey which, if it did not exist, would have to be imagined. A staircase with good stucco-work, a library, but above all the Abbot's Room with Troger at work once more and again upon the ceiling, and let into the walls a series of monastic scenes of monks in white robes by Magnasco. This is indeed almost too good to be true. One had never thought to find his monkish fantasies in an actual monastery. The paintings could not be improved upon either for their intrinsic excellence or appropriate setting. And, last of all, Wilhering, just outside Linz. Wilhering is altogether exceptional in Austria for being not Baroque but Rococo, and graceful and fanciful as any building of the kind in Bavaria. Pulpit and choir organ of exquisite quality, and the door frames as magical in their gracefulness as the run of ornament in an early violin sonata by Mozart. Wilhering is a place in which to learn to appreciate the Rococo. It must always come as a shock to Anglo-Saxons to find the whole interior of an abbey church treated with the imaginative delicacy of a Chippendale mirror frame, not excluding its leanings to *chinoiserie*, and carried out in more than one tone of gold, and colours.

Linz, the biggest of these Danube towns, with St Florian and Wilhering so near by, and only marred by its associations with the most dreadful being in European history, is a place for a stay of several days. From Linz a road leads to Steyr on the river Enns, with many old houses in its market place. On top of the Sonntagberg, a mountain not far from Steyr and near Waidhofen an der Ybbs, is a pilgrimage church, unknown to the writer, but from all accounts one of the masterpieces of Austrian Baroque. It has a beautiful pulpit and organ case, and an immense fresco by Daniel Gran which is that painter's finest work. From Steyr the road continues due south, past Admont, another but a disappointing Abbey, in the direction of the Austrian lakes. It may rain here nearly as frequently as at Salzburg but it will be a warmer rain than at the English lakes. Gmunden lies at the head of all the lakes, and Ischl at the centre, the preferred resort of the two, because of the delayed action in its air. Kaiser Franz-Josef might still be staying in his summer villa, and it would come as no surprise to see the familiar figure of Strauss walking through the gardens to the Kurhaus with the peculiar and springing step so indicative of his genius as he takes up his violin to conduct the orchestra a moment or two later. On the first occasion I went to Ischl I sat at the next table at luncheon to two old ladies, the daughters of the Prince Metternich who had been Ambassador in Paris during the Second

Empire. Their mother was the famous Princess Metternich, friend of the Empress Eugénie, and one may read in memoirs of how her good-looking, fair-bearded husband was a beautiful waltz player, and how Eugénie appeared in a huge yellow crinoline at the ball at which both Strauss and Waldteufel led their dance orchestras, given by the Metternichs in Paris. Those are ghostly memories of a long dead epoch. Not so a session at Zauner's, which must be the foremost confectioner in Europe, and where a particular, if unlikely, marriage of wild strawberry with chocolate gives a lasting memory to the summer day.

Being no lake lover, what am I to say of the Austrian Lake District? That the Weisses Rössl, no other than 'The White Horse Inn' of waltz fame, is at St Wolfang on the Wolfgang-See, and that everyone, or nearly everyone, knows who was given Wolfgang Amadeus for his Christian names? What is beautiful is the high altar at St Wolfgang, a winged altar painting by Michael Pacher, its carved portions even better than the painted, all in all a fifteenth-century masterpiece in a land where not much, and that much not very good, is of this early date. More apt to the Austrian temperament is the 'fisher-pulpit' at Traunkirchen, on the Traunsee, a pulpit in the form of a boat draped with fishing nets, on a base of gilded icicles with apostles holding oars or rudders. Up above upon the canopy there is a more than life-sized lobster; or is it a crayfish? Another of the 'fisher-pulpits' is at a little village called Irsee, near Kaufbeuren, in Bavaria. This is yet more fanciful, at least in its upper part; the front of a ship with sail and foremast, with cupids minding the sail and manning the yards.

It must always be an excitement to arrive at Salzburg, a town of just the right size of population, and of which the spirit is typified in the lovely Mirabell Garden with its statues and espaliered and clipped trees. If one has not been to Italy, there is the touch of Italy at Salzburg, and yet one has to admit that it could not be more Austrian. How can one ever forget first coming here? The soft and gentle Austrian speech and manner after the German; the schillings instead of marks; the Italianate churches; the first visit to the shop where they sell *dirndls*? My own memories of Salzburg are of the first musical festival in 1923; of being taken by Alban Berg to see Schönberg in a villa on one of the lakes; of meeting Adolf Loos, a well-known architect, friend of Kokoschka, and connected with the Vienna *Sezession*; and of being embraced, 'Kiss-of-Beethoven' fashion, by Janáček after a performance of some of his music. And I remember, also, the old lady in the hotel, so old that she fell asleep in the dining-room, watching the dancing. She was an Austrian baroness, ninety-three years old, and the niece of Meyerbeer, for whom she had kept house in Paris, so that she must have often heard Chopin play. Haydn quartets were played to us under a white Meissen chandelier in the banqueting hall at Leopoldskron, where Reinhardt lived; and coming fresh to it from Italy it was inevitable that one was disappointed by the waterworks in the garden at Hellbrunn and found them trite

16

VI RATTENBERG AM INN

and jejune after Tivoli and Frascati, as, also, the horse paintings in the Marstall or Summer Riding School of the Prince-Archbishops. On the other hand the Italianate churches of Salzburg, one or two of them by Fischer von Erlach, are delightful.

There are complaints that Austria is small, but in fact it seems very large indeed because of the extent to which it is cut up by mountains. Carinthia is a long way removed from Salzburg. It could be said to consist of scenery and water sports on the Wörther-See for there is little else to do. Fine architecture has vanished for the moment and there is not even a 'fisher-pulpit'. But it is difficult to be anywhere in Austria without musical associations. Brahms began his Second Symphony and wrote most of his Violin Concerto during summer holidays on two successive years at Pörtschach on the Wörther-See. In Carinthia one feels the proximity of another and different world of human beings, and Slovenia with Lake Bled lies only an hour or two away over the Karawanken. Styria, next province to Carinthia and sounding unfamiliar, as Steiermark, fills the gap on the map between Hungary and the Burgenland, but I have not visited Styria and do not therefore write of it further than to say that the architectural ban is lifted there but to no great purpose, though Graz has Italianate buildings—of the seventeenth century which is an indeterminate date in Germanic countries—and that the work of an architect with a name like Pietro de Pomis looks to be less promising than it sounds.

But neither is Vorarlberg, the province at the far Western end of Austria abutting on Lake Constance, of any interest in this respect. Indeed, Vorarlberg is almost a waste of time with the Tyrol so near to hand. For the Tyrol is perhaps the most fascinating mountain land in Europe with all things to do with it strange and fantastic from the costumes downwards. Even Kitzbühel, which might seem unlikely, has a pretty church interior in a district where all is winter sports and vociferous with ski-ing expressions. But there must still be mountain valleys that are unspoilt, with marvellous air and scenery, the old peasant hospitality, and costumes as strange and bizarre as can be imagined. The pattern of such a valley, but on a big scale and perhaps spoilt now, is the Zillertal where till not long ago all things were original, including a race of striped cattle like the 'Old Gloucesters' in the park at Badminton, said only to occur elsewhere in Europe on a former estate in Poland. And there are villages, remoter still on the Swiss border, where the curious Ladin or Romantsch may yet be spoken. Before this last war, at least, there were farmers to be seen even in the streets of Innsbruck, smoking their long pipes, who were as hirsute and odd in costume as any long-haired Breton peasant. And it is to Innsbruck that we now turn our attention, a town with mountains towering high above roof level at the end of nearly every street.

A town in a wonderful situation so near to both Italy and Germany—but no, that is not quite true because there is the huge extent of the South Tyrol, still largely German speaking,

VII THE LECHTAL ALPS IN THE BREGENZERWALD REGION

with gradual descent through Merano and Bolzano down to Lake Garda and Verona, or through the red Dolomites to Venice. Therefore, Innsbruck is not really so near to Italy as it might seem to be. It could be said that it is neither German nor Italian, and certainly not Viennese, but Tyrolese, with national characteristics going far back to the fourteenth century or earlier. But Innsbruck and the Tyrol are inseparably associated with the Kaiser Maximilian I (1493–1519). Let us look for a moment at the *Hunting* and *Fishing Books* of Maximilian, records written down at his dictation, with paintings by Jörg Kölderer of Innsbruck which are entirely redolent of the Tyrol. The *Hunting Book* opens with the report of his chief huntsmen upon the two hundred beats where chamois were to be found. Obviously, chamois were less rare than now. A stag stands at bay at a wood's edge with his does behind him. The scene is a high mountain valley with the pine trees half into the snow. Lower down, a mountain stream of a vivid blueness runs over the shingle, and a stag swims in the deeper water. Maximilian on his white horse, between two halberdiers, fires his crossbow. Or it is a snowy defile, and the chamois with stags on their heels are leaping upon the snowy hillsides.

The *Fishing Book*, to continue with this breath of air from the mountains, is no less enchanting. There is a picture of the Long Meadow outside Innsbruck, with fir-clad hills, birds on the wing, and fishing in progress in a dam, with a wooden house that has a pair of antlers on its gables. In another painting there are mounted knights with feathered hats in red and white, and a fishing lodge with balconies and wooden slatted roof. Or trout fishing is in progress in a little pool, and the particular race of trout for which the lake was famous are distinguished by the bright red spots upon their skins. There is even a scene of crayfishing by torchlight, under a castle, with a four-horse waggon carrying a barrel for the catch. In another and last picture, for we must dally here no longer, huntsmen and peasants are dancing to the music of a rustic band. These little pictures, better than anything else, give the special and historical characteristics of the Tyrol.

After admiring them, or only hearing of them, it is imperative to go to the Hofkirche of Innsbruck and look at the statues of knights and paladins around Maximilian's tomb. The figure of King Arthur, the most famous of the bronze statues, with the ends of his moustache coming over the edges of his visor, has an extraordinary prophetic resemblance to an Englishman; to, say, any officer of the Brigade of Guards who fought in the Egyptian or Boer Wars. The statues in question are not great works of art, but they are of curious effect because of their elaborate armour, the princely crowns or diadems of many of them, and high Habsburg noses. It is impossible, also, not to look with some degree of admiration at the Goldenes Dachl, the Gothic balcony with gilded copper roof, where Maximilian appeared in public. Nearby is the Rokoko Haus, which until you look into it more closely could be one of Gaudí's *nouveau art* apartment houses in Barcelona. Perhaps antithesis in taste could not be better expressed than in installing a sculpture in bronze or marble by Henry Moore beside Maximilian's tomb.

Sensations of how different a sort are to be experienced in a convent church at Hall, a few miles from Innsbruck, where is the most extraordinary collection imaginable of saints' skeletons robed by the nuns in 'Spanish' court dress, with diamond ornaments and hooped skirts, or long waisted surcoats and swords by their sides! It is of a jewelled morbidity that would have fascinated Baudelaire. A skeleton or two, one would surmise, must have been disarticulated, or entirely taken to pieces, in order to get them into the elegant poses of reclining on an elbow, or lying only half-asleep and dreaming, which the nuns required of them before they could begin dressing the skeletons. The nuns' macabre needlework is lavished upon this Dance of Death, and it indeed verges more upon theatrical than religious art. For an antidote we can go to Stams, a Cistercian abbey not far away. Its snowy interior of a marvellous gaiety makes one wonder why it was that no rose-pink church interior, nor yet one in daffodil yellow or pistache green, was ever achieved by architects in the age of Rococo. The same query comes to mind in seeing the inevitable, and invariable blue and white *azulejos* (tiles) in Portugal. But colour as a leading principle in building seems only to have been practised by the Persians, and its examples are at Meshed, Isfahan and Samarkand.

Having glanced, however hurriedly, at much of what is interesting and characteristic of Austria, there now remains the summing-up and judgement on what are its distinctive features and what it all amounts to. First of all, Austria may be, now, but it never was before, a small country of largely Alpine features with a huge city of some two million inhabitants (Vienna) attaching to it at one end. But because the Habsburg possessions came to them through marriage, and not from conquest, it is perhaps true that the Austrians inherited their great position and did not have in them the characteristics of a 'master race'. Yet the white coats of the Austrian soldiers were, formerly, as familiar a sight on battlefields as the red coats of the British; just as the Habsburg family, now looked on—and very wrongly—as a symbol of aristocratic decadence, produced in the very odd-looking Archduke Charles one of the few generals except Wellington who ever defeated Napoleon. The political record of the Austrians was bad in Bohemia, though no worse than that of our countrymen in Ireland. Neither was it good in Italy, where it is a historical humiliation to think of the Austrians as masters of the Venetian Republic, 'La Serenissima', however weak and feeble the Venetians had become. Neither does there seem reason for the Habsburgs succeeding in Tuscany to the Medicis; and they held Milan and Modena, and often interfered in Naples. I am great-nephew of an old lady, now dead, who while in Italy with her parents when she was five years old, had witnessed a street fight in Milan between the followers of Garibaldi and the Austrian whitecoats. The redshirts won, and one

21

of them, seeing that she was an English child and knowing that English sympathy lay with the rebels, tore off his red cockade and pinned it to her dress. I have been shown that red cockade, and held it in my hand; and no doubt had I been alive at the time would have sympathized with the English workmen who chased Field-Marshal Radetzky out of Barclay's Brewery. Whether, in the light of what has happened since, any good at all has come from the unification of Italy is another matter, for it is true that hardly an Italian of eminence has been born since 1870.

Also, it is lamentably true that this former Empire whose greatest men were musicians, has failed in this channel, or, at least, the springs of inspiration have run dry. All that is left is Vienna, and a handful of monasteries, and the beautiful mountains and the countryside. The period of her greatness has little or nothing to do with the German Renaissance, and except for the links between Kaiser Maximilian and Albrecht Dürer, Austria is in no sense the land of Luther and Melanchthon, any more than it has connexion with Handel or Johann Sebastian Bach. Austria is essentially a land of the Counter-Reformation, but there is more evidence of this in Prague than there is in Vienna itself. When Prince Eugen and the Archduke Charles and Metternich are nearly forgotten, there will be—her musicians apart—monasteries like Melk and St Florian to remember, and as relics of her former historical greatness the regalia of the Holy Roman Empire in the Schatzkammer in Vienna. The robes and crown of Charlemagne are no less genuine because they are really Sicilian and the regalia of later, Norman kings. Their value is, even, more poetical than intrinsic, as Hohenstaufen and Habsburg in the charnel house of history become merged together in historic time. Now, in our day, Mozart and Beethoven are the fame of Austria and it is forgiven and forgotten that the former was buried in a pauper's grave. Nature stays beautiful in her lakes and mountain pastures, while in abbeys like Wilhering and Seitenstetten we discover that music is not Austria's only greatness and that there is this architectural forerunner and prelude to her golden age.

SACHEVERELL SITWELL
December, 1958

THE PLATES

WIEN, ST. STEPHAN

WIEN, ST. STEPHAN

WIEN, KIRCHE DER BARMHERZIGEN BRÜDER

3

WIEN, BELVEDERE

WIEN, PRINZ EUGEN

5

WIEN, OBERES BELVEDERE

6

WIEN, BELVEDERE

WIEN, HOFBURG 8

WIEN, HOFREITSCHULE 9

WIEN, HOFREITSCHULE

WIEN, HOFBIBLIOTHEK

WIEN, GROSSER MUSIKVEREINSSAAL

12

WIENER SÄNGERKNABEN

13

WIEN, STAATSOPER 14

WIEN, STAATSOPER 15

WIEN, STAATSOPER «DER ROSENKAVALIER»

16

WIEN, STADTPARK, JOHANN STRAUSS

WIEN, STADTPARK 18

WIENER WALZER 19

WIEN, BURGTHEATER 20

WIEN, BALLHAUSPLATZ 21

WIEN, KARLSKIRCHE

WIEN, RINGTURM

IEN, MÖLKERBASTEI, BEETHOVENHAUS

EILIGENSTÄDTER BEETHOVENHAUS

WIEN, BAROCKMUSEUM, MARIA THERESIA

KLOSTERNEUBURG

STIFT HEILIGENKREUZ

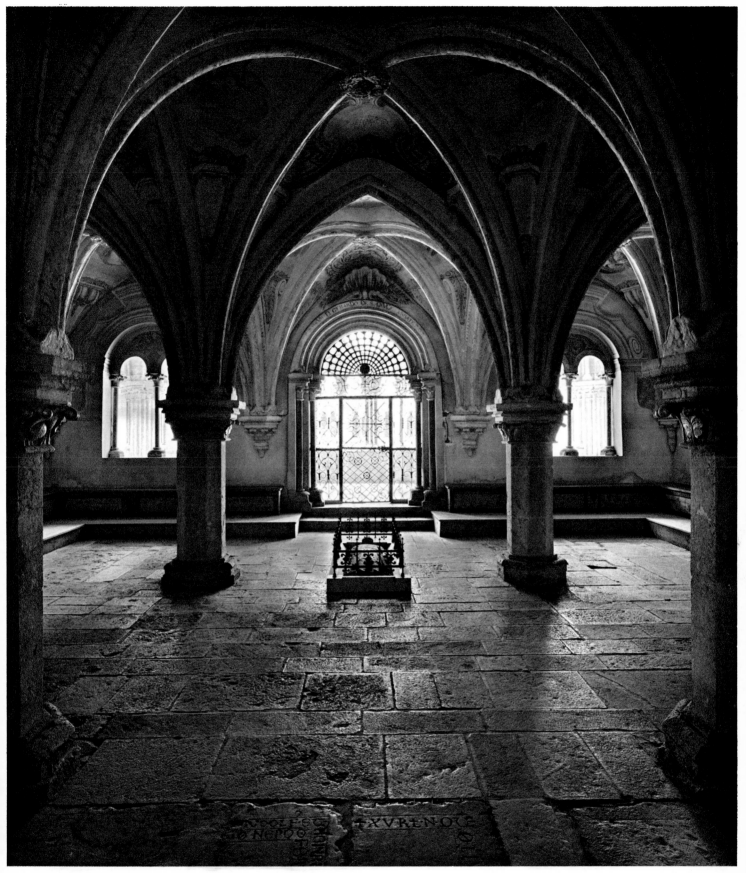

STIFT HEILIGENKREUZ

NEUSIEDLERSEE

BURG GÜSSING

EISENSTADT, SCHLOSS ESTERHAZY

EISENSTADT, WOHNHAUS JOSEPH HAYDNS   36

WEINBAUERNHOF BEI TRAUSDORF

37

TRAUSDORF AN DER WULKA

38

BURG FORCHTENSTEIN

BURG LOCKENHAUS

URG RAPPOTTENSTEIN, GOTISCHE VORHALLE

SCHÖNGRABERN, PFARRKIRCHE

SCHÖNGRABERN, PFARRKIRCHE

ZWETTL

STIFT ZWETTL

4

STIFT ALTENBURG

STIFT ALTENBURG

STIFT GÖTTWEIG

ST. PÖLTEN, DOMKIRCHE

PÖCHLARN   54

LOIBEN   55

STEIN-KREMS

STEIN-KREMS

WACHAU, DONAU

DÜRNSTEIN

DÜRNSTEIN

ST. MICHAEL

DONAU

WEISSENKIRCHEN, TEISSENHOFER HOF

WACHAU, WEINLESE

66

MAUER BEI MELK

PERSENBEUG AN DER DONAU

SCHLOSS SCHALLABURG

SCHLOSS SCHÖNBÜHEL AN DER DONAU

MELK

MELK, STIFTSKIRCHE

MELK, STIFTSBIBLIOTHEK 74

ABTEI SEITENSTETTEN, KAISERSTIEGE   75

ABTEI SEITENSTETTEN 76

ST. FLORIAN, BRUCKNER-ORGEL

LINZ AN DER DONAU

STEYR, STADTPLATZ

STEYR, SGRAFFITOHAUS

KREMSMÜNSTER, GÜNTHER-HOCHGRAB

TASSILO-KELCH

KREMSMÜNSTER, FISCHBEHÄLTER

ORT BEI GMUNDEN

SCHLOSS IN ORT

HALLSTATT

HALLSTÄTTER SEE, FRONLEICHNAM

TRAUNKIRCHEN, FISCHER-KANZEL

BRAUNAU AM INN

HALLEIN AM INN

GOSAUSEE MIT DACHSTEIN

ST. GILGEN AM WOLFGANGSEE

ST. WOLFGANG

SALZBURG

ALZBURG, MIRABELLGARTEN UND FESTUNG

SALZBURG

SALZBURG, DOMFASSADE

SALZBURG, FELSENREITSCHULE

SALZBURG, ST. PETER

SALZBURG, MOZART-HAUS

SALZBURG, RESIDENZ

BAD GASTEIN

ZELLERSEE

ENNSTALER ALPEN

STIFT ADMONT

DER STEIRISCHE ERZBERG

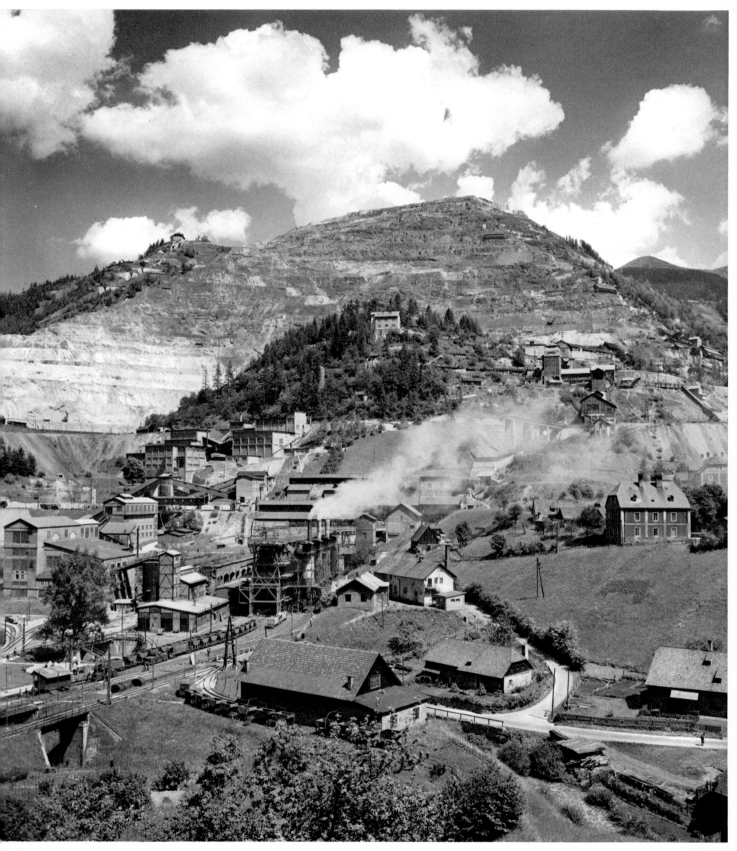

LEOPOLDSTEINER SEE

BRUCK AN DER MUR, KORNMESSERHAUS

BRUCK AN DER MUR

BURG SCHLAINING

FESTE RIEGERSBURG

GRAZ, LANDESZEUGHAUS

GRAZ

STIFT ST. LAMBRECHT

GRAZ, LANDHAUS-HOF

FRIESACH

ST. VEIT AN DER GLAN, RATHAUS

BURG HOCHOSTERWITZ

BURG NEUDENSTEIN

MARIA WÖRTH

RUINE GRIFFEN MIT KARAWANKEN

KLAGENFURT, LANDHAUS

SCHLOSS BAYERHOFEN

STRASSBURG IM GURKTAL 14

GURKER DOM 14

GURKER DOM

GURKER DOM

HEILIGENBLUT

GROSSGLOCKNER

ERZHERZOG-JOHANN-HÜTTE

GROSSGLOCKNERSTRASSE

KAPRUN

SCHLOSS MÜNICHAU MIT KAISERGEBIRGE 152

KITZBÜHEL 15

DER WILDE KAISER

INNTAL / ZILLERTAL

ZILLERTAL / FINKENBERG 15

ZILLERTAL 15

SOLBAD HALL

SOLBAD HALL

INNSBRUCK

INNSBRUCK, DAS GOLDENE DACHL

INNSBRUCK, ROKOKOHAUS   166

KALVARIENBERG BEI ARZL 16

PESTKAPELLE BEI SCHATTWALD 17

EHRWALD MIT ZUGSPITZE

ÖTZ

ÖTZTAL, SEELENFERNER BRUCH

IMSTER SCHEMENLAUFEN

INNBRÜCKE BEI ROPPEN

SCHLOSS NAUDERSBERG

178

LANDSCHAFT BEI IMST

SCHUHPLATTLER

RANGLER-TANZ

BALZTANZ

LECH AM ARLBERG

18

VALLUGAGRAT

ARLBERG

MONTAFON, TSCHAGGUNSER MITTAGSSPITZE

MONTAFON, BLICK VOM KAPPELLJOCH ZUR TSCHAGGUNSER MITTAGSSPITZE

FELDKIRCH

BREGENZER WALD

BREGENZ

HISTORICAL NOTES

THE FEDERAL REPUBLIC OF AUSTRIA

HANS BERNHARD

Present-day Austria came into being after the First World War, when the old Habsburg Empire had totally disintegrated. The basic structure of the new State was decided by the Peace of St Germain in 1919. Subsequently, from 1938 to 1945, she formed a part of the Third Reich, and after 1945 there followed difficult years of military occupation. At last, on May 15, 1955, the longed-for treaty of liberation was finally ratified by the Foreign Ministers of the United States, Russia, France and Austria. After seventeen years the Second Republic, as the country had styled itself since its emancipation from Nazism, was empowered to direct its own fortunes.

Modern Austria faces several disadvantages inherent in the old Danube kingdom from which she originated. Only a tiny Alpine State remains of the former mighty empire stretching to the Alps, the Carpathians, the Sudetenland and the Karstland. Northwards from the Danube it penetrates the Bohemian Massif; and at the Neusiedlersee it touches on the plain of Hungary; otherwise the country's 30,766 sq. miles lie in the eastern Alps and in their northern and eastern approaches. This is a determining factor with regard to climate, vegetation, spread of population, and the individual nature of Austria's economy. Nevertheless, the conception of Austria as 'an Alpine country' is only partially justified; for the main bulk of the population is found, not in the mountain regions, but along the Danube valley, along the outer rim of the Pannonian Basin, and beyond the Danube. And even more important than the actual density of population is the difference in *types* of inhabitants.

The open spaces of the river-basins and plains have set a stamp on those who have settled there which differentiates them from their compatriots whose homes lie in the hemmed-in mountain valleys. For centuries these Alpine-dwellers have traditionally followed their own paths, and in addition have vigorously preserved their native way of life, thus contributing much to the special character of the Austrian Federation. Again, the many aspects of Austrian culture have their roots in her geographical differences and in the diversity of types of men produced by these differences.

The physical shape of the country is not at all satis-factory. For to the west of the line Braunau–Salzburg–Lienz the width of eastern Austria is suddenly whittled down. The Tyrol and the Vorarlberg lie like narrow outcrops on the outer edge of the main territory. A distance of 340 miles separates the middle reaches of the Danube from the Rhine. But at its narrowest point Austria measures only twenty-five miles across. One main railway line links east and west. The tortuous frontier and the break-up of the former railway network constructed in the days of the old Habsburg monarchy have combined to introduce the so-called corridor trains, which travel (with locked doors) out of Austria across stretches of foreign territory and so into Austria again. This happens, for instance, on the line from Lienz over the Italian Pustertal and the Brenner Pass to Innsbruck; or from here via Garmisch–Partenkirchen to the Lechtal and the surround-ing districts. Austria is encircled by seven countries—Germany, Czechoslovakia, Hungary, Yugoslavia, Italy, Switzerland and Liechtenstein. And these many frontiers have little natural protection, for the all-too-rare belts of flat land lie for the most part in these border zones: to the east where Austria meets Hungary (the area known as the Burgenland), on the Danube, in the Rhine valley, in the Vorarlberg and on the Yugoslav frontier. Particularly disadvantageous is the unusual situation of the capital so near to the eastern border.

Notwithstanding its small area, Austria is a country of many contrasts. This has come about naturally with the political growth of the Republic. Modern Austria has evolved from a union of several small independent States, a union which—with the exception of Salzburg—was effected centuries ago. These federal provinces, as they are called, have, despite long adherence to the empire,

preserved many of their individual characteristics. They therefore form a convenient basis for describing the country as it is now.

Federal Provinces	Area in sq. miles	Population 1951	Density of Population
Vorarlberg	1,004	193,657	193
Tyrol	4,790	427,465	89
Salzburg	2,762	327,232	118
Styria	6,327	1,109,335	175
Carinthia	3,679	474,764	129
Upper Austria	4,622	1,108,720	240
Lower Austria	7,397	1,461,655	198
Vienna (1954)	160	1,616,125	10,101
Burgenland	1,530	276,136	180

A short tour of these provinces, approximately in the order in which they appear in this book, will lead us to a closer understanding of Austria's different aspects, though our remarks must necessarily be brief. From the geographical point of view, two main types of scenery occur: one in the area lying principally in the eastern Alps, the other in the neighbouring, mostly flatter frontier regions. The non-alpine areas included in the Second Republic comprise the country east of the Alps, with the Danube valley, the Bohemian Massif and the border zone touching on the plain of Hungary.

From the Bavarian Plateau the alpine approaches sweep down into Austria along a wide front. East of Regensburg, however, the Bohemian Massif draws steadily nearer to the alpine ridge, gradually compressing this 'foreland' as we shall call it, until at Melk it is no more than $4\frac{1}{4}$ miles wide. It opens out again beyond the eastern end of the Massif, into the Vienna Basin.

This foreland is gently undulating, generally hilly country, and very fertile. The former layer of pliocene rock has been largely eroded, only traces of it being preserved, as at Hausruck and Kobenserwald. At the mouths of the Inn, Traun and Enns valleys the melting waters of the Ice Age glaciers have carried huge deposits of this rock as far as the Danube itself, deposits which had originally been pushed by the cascading alpine streams to the foot of the Bohemian Massif. This age-old formation, partly composed of weathered granite and gneiss, with peaks rising to between 1,500 and 2,400 ft above sea level, has in the course of time become a landscape criss-crossed with narrow valleys. The Danube Basin presents an amazing variety of contrasting scenery, and is frequently compared with the Rhine below Mainz. Sometimes the great river winds along steep-sided valleys, as for instance below Passau, Freinberg and Ardagger, at Grein and between Melk and Spitz; elsewhere it flows through broad fertile plains. The towns which have grown up along its banks remind us that this is one of the ancient trade-routes, while its numerous old castles testify to the troubles and insecurity of past ages.

The sweep of country between the south-easterly ridge of the Alps and the Czech and German frontiers in the north comprises Upper and Lower Austria. Though they have many common characteristics, these two provinces are basically different. One belongs rather to the alpine region, the other to the Pannonian Basin. Furthermore, we must take positions *vis-à-vis* Vienna into consideration. They ought therefore to be treated as separate regions, as should the Burgenland, another area with a character all its own.

VIENNA is a State in itself. The heavy concentration of population in so small an area—10,100 inhabitants to the square mile—the almost complete absence of those trades and professions that are concerned with agriculture, and a citizenry drawn from many different races: these are the hall-marks of this great metropolis.

Vienna was originally built on the right bank of the Danube, on a raised, dry, shelf of land by the river. It was first of all a Celtic settlement, and later became a Roman cantonment with the name of Vindobona. By the Middle Ages the city, under the Babenbergs and Habsburgs, had ineluctably evolved as the focal point of European politics, culture and learning. In 1804 it had become the capital city of the newly founded Austrian Empire. A hundred years ago the old city walls collapsed, and in their place the Ringstrasse was built; 187 ft wide and nearly 2½ miles long, it is one of the most beautiful thoroughfares in the world. And when in 1890 another outer wall was pulled down, the Gürtel, or Girdle, was constructed as a second demarcation line in the plan of modern Vienna.

The city's position for trade is probably unique. From the Rhone valley to the Ukraine there is only one point which affords completely free access from the Baltic to the Adriatic, and it lies here, at the eastern edge of the long curve of the Alps. In addition, the sudden narrowing of the alpine foreland between the northern limestone Alps, or Kalkalpen, and the Bohemian Massif forces traffic between West and East into the Vienna Basin. Vienna grew in importance as the home of the powerful merchant princes: but her greater rôle was that of a mediating power between east and west, a bulwark against the encroaching steppe-dwellers of the Near East, and, not least, a guardian of western culture (1529 and 1683), a task whose fulfilment has won her undying fame.

The split-up of the Danube kingdom was a severe and painful setback for the aspiring metropolis. Almost overnight she was bereft of her central position, and found herself set instead at the fringe of a small mountainous state. There she stood, an industrial colossus backed by a sparsely populated hinterland, with customs barriers only twenty-five to thirty-seven miles from her gates. But, for all that, Vienna still holds the key position of the whole land area between the Alps and the Carpathians—an extraordinary advantage in times of peaceful trade. Of Vienna's inhabitants 75 per cent are supported by her industries, trade and commerce. Furthermore, Vienna, 'reflecting Austria's keen interest in every aspect of culture, ranks second only to Paris as an arbiter in all questions of good taste', and her artistic prowess, more particularly in the world of music, has scarcely been surpassed—we have only to think of Haydn, Mozart, Beethoven, Schubert, Bruckner, Brahms, Strauss and Lehar.

A brief tour of the city leads us first of all to the 'Steffel', the tower of St Stephen's Cathedral, Vienna's most striking landmark, which dominates not only by its outward appearance, but because of its many associations with the past. The 'Steffel' is very dear to Viennese hearts. Other places of interest are the Archbishop's Palace and the House of the Order of Teutonic Knights. The crypt of the Church of the Capucins, near the Neuer Markt, where the Habsburgs lie in their royal tombs is well worth a visit. On the Ringstrasse are situated the University, the Town Hall, the Parliament building, and Law Courts, the National Library, the Museum for Natural History and the History of Art, the State Opera House and many fine churches. Vienna possesses a splendid array of fine buildings, almost all recalling the atmosphere of earlier centuries. Between the Gürtel and the Ring suburbs have grown up, and still farther out, mingling with what were once vintners' villages, we find more suburbs with large tenement-style houses.

THE BURGENLAND is ancient frontier country. Coveted by one enemy power after another, it was forever being ravaged by invading armies, torn asunder by warring states, and then fortified anew. Thanks to the fact that the greater part of its population is German-speaking, the victors ceded it to Austria in 1919. Ödenburg, allowed to determine its own future, chose to become part of Hungary, though by a relatively small majority of votes. This meant that the already narrow province was now only a few miles wide at Forchtenau.

Apart from occasional mountain spurs, the Burgenland is mostly rolling hill-country, though in the neighbourhood of the Neusiedlersee, twenty-two miles long but only a few feet deep, it becomes quite flat and steppe-like.

Almost half the population is engaged in agriculture, the main crops being wheat, rye, barley, oats and maize. The area between the lake, the Rosaliengebirge and the Leithagebirge is famous for its fruit. Rust and Eisenstadt produce a great deal of wine, while around the Neusied-lersee a wide area is devoted to vegetable-growing, and thick groves of Spanish chestnuts cluster along the foothills of the Rosaliengebirge. The Burgenland exports consider-able amounts of produce, and the inhabitants of the nearby cities of Vienna and Graz derive special benefit from its proximity.

Racially and linguistically, the Burgenland is far and away less unified than the rest of Austria. But the cold seclusion of the adjacent Russian satellite countries, with their barbed-wire entanglements and customs barriers, has reorientated the province, economically speaking, towards the West, thus contributing to a more rapid awakening of racial consciousness.

LOWER AUSTRIA, together with Vienna, orig-inally formed the nucleus of the old Danube monarchy. Today it is a small frontier zone, touching on all the major geographical regions of Austria–Hungary. Fertile tertiary soil with loess, flat, sometimes marshy plains and scree-covered granite belts alternate with arid, pine-clad rock strata and barren plateaux. In agricultural production, Lower Austria far exceeds every other province in the Republic. Its crops of wheat, rye, maize, potatoes, sugar beet, fruit and wine are very large, and the area is an in-dispensable source of supply for the huge population of Vienna. Its woodlands, too, cover an amazingly large area, so that the north-westerly corner of the province is best described as a forest zone. Naturally enough, therefore, the timber industry occupies the leading place. Where minerals are concerned, no less than 99 per cent of Austria's total coal output is mined here, whilst petroleum is produced on the eastern edge of the wine-growing district.

The Vienna Basin is an 'inroad' caused by geological changes in the sector between the Alps and the Car-pathians. Small earth tremors indicate that these changes may even yet be incomplete, and thermal springs have appeared to substantiate this theory.

One third of Austria's industries are located in the Vienna Basin; indeed, these are partly dependent on Vienna's own heavy industries. From the point of view of commerce it is admirably situated. Trade routes open out in every direction—via Hainburg, Bruck on the Leitha and Ebenfurth to Hungary and the Balkans; the Danube and the Vienna–St Pölten railway connect with the west; the Semmering Pass leads south to the Adriatic; and the old Bernsteinstrasse (Amber route) along the river March runs north towards the Baltic. Wiener Neustadt has made a good recovery after the devastations of war, and has plunged with fresh energy into industrial expansion.

North of the Danube and east of the Manhartsberg lies the famous wine-producing region, the Weinviertel, a uniform stretch of hilly country rising to between 900 and 1,200 ft above sea level. Here the warm dry summers and not-too-severe winters permit widespread viticulture and even larger yields of wheat, maize and barley. Vienna's fresh milk supply also comes from this district. On the eastern edge of the Weinviertel, at Zisterdorf, the first petroleum wells were drilled in 1930, and two years later petroleum was discovered at a depth of over 4,000 ft. The yearly output of between three and three-and-a-half million tons is worth over a billion Austrian shillings.

The alpine foreland penetrates only a little way into Lower Austria, as has already been pointed out. It consists largely of loess on broken rock-strata, providing fine arable land. St Pölten, important as a railway junction, occupies a central position in this province, though its nearness to

190

Vienna prevents its further development into a city of comparable size.

Our journey through Lower Austria would be incomplete without a brief glimpse of the Vienna Woods. The western side of this fertile hill-country, with its many valleys, was brought under cultivation in early times by Frankish settlers. In the former Imperial game reserves and in those parts of the forest attached to various monasteries, the woods have retained their legendary beauty. The Viennese appreciate only too well the value of this green oasis on their doorstep, though nowadays more and more villas are springing up along its wooded vales.

UPPER AUSTRIA. The region between the Inn and the Enns, together with the country north of the Danube has, after Vienna, the greatest density of population in the whole republic—240 to the square mile. This is primarily due to its widespread economic development.

The Salzkammergut, with its many lakes, its spa at Bad Ischl, its Wolfgansee and its Dachstein Mountains, is a well-known tourist centre and, as the name suggests, its salt-mines are also important. The discovery of a number of inhumation and cinerary graves—relics of the Celtic 'Hallstatt civilization'—bears witness to the very early colonization of the region. At the time of the great migrations the salt-mines must have been abandoned—not to be reopened until the beginning of the fourteenth century. Hallein, Ischl, Aussee and Hallstatt are the principal towns, and Austria's largest salt-works is at Ebensee. The region of the Kalkalpen, separating the Salzkammergut from the Enns, is thinly populated, though iron, timber, textiles, fruit and clay are still produced on a small scale. The rafts which used to ferry iron ore and timber down the Enns have long since disappeared, and today highly mechanized traffic thunders through the tranquil valleys.

Steyr, lying between the River Steyr and the Enns, was the largest city in Austria about 1600. Ore from the Erzberg was brought by water to Steyr at little cost, and the river was alive with small craft, ferrying the precious minerals. Imposing mansions in the Gothic and Baroque styles adorn the old part of the town. After 1918 her armaments factories were turned over to the manufacture of automobiles. Steyr also produces motor-cycles, tractors and machine tools.

A more notable city is Linz on the Danube, with a population of 200,000. Its already favourable situation with regard to trade was enhanced by the development of the railway network, and the way was clear for Linz to mushroom to importance as a great industrial centre. Iron is transported by rail, while coal from Germany is ferried via Linz down the Danube, which carries its heavy freight on its long journey to the sea. Forty thousand men are employed by the heavy industrial group known as United Austrian Iron and Steelworks Ltd (Vereinigte Österreichische Eisen- und Stahlwerke A.G., or VOEST). The new enlarged harbour on the Danube handles the steadily increasing output of goods, and a productive shipyard builds ships of up to 2,000 tons. The construction of the Rhine–Main–Danube canal, a project first envisaged by Charlemagne, would make Linz a commercial city of international status.

Let us pay a brief visit to the 'Mühlviertel', the region beyond the Danube, where the granite hills are furrowed by steep valleys. 'These valleys are often so narrow that while it is possible to look across from one village to its opposite number and read the time from a clock-tower there, an hour's walk may well separate the two.' This area, originally settled in a somewhat haphazard fashion by peoples of Slavic descent, later underwent intensive colonization by Germanic tribes. Many of the place-names point to the systematic cultivation of the woodland stretches, and to this day timber is felled in large quantities. The fertile soil yields crops of potatoes, rye, oats and flax, and at one time linen was exported from here to Italy, Hungary and the Balkans.

Upper Austria produces 25 per cent of the country's total exports—a fine example of what can be done to exploit the economic potentialities of a region possessing few raw materials or fuel supplies (even electric current has to be tapped from outside). The only mineral deposits of any significance are of lignite, kaolin and bauxite.

The predominantly alpine provinces of Austria comprise Styria, Carinthia, Salzburg, the Tyrol and the Vorarlberg.

Austria is a land of mountains; but of these the eastern Alps are less imposing than the western Alps, and are consequently more open, more accessible and more habitable, especially along their wide valleys. One impressive example of this type of long, straight valley is that which follows the route Inn–Salzach–Enns–Mur–Mürz–Semmering; another, in the south, is the Lienz–Drau valley. These break up the alpine massif into a crystalline central region, with 'Kalkalpen' to north and south which in their turn divide up into numerous subsidiary mountain chains of varying size. From this brief topographical outline it will be clear that—quite apart from the varying geological characteristics of the several provinces—this is a country of widely differing scenery, and one that presents violent contrasts. These geological and geographical peculiarities have made the region a tourists' paradise; but they have also endowed it with the rich mineral deposits and warm springs that have brought renown to its spas. The eastern Alps offer considerable variations of climate, too, primarily because of their differing height above sea level, but also due to the degree of exposure to the prevailing winds. Thus, in the valleys to the north and west a predominantly Central European type of climate prevails, while the valleys running east possess marked Pannonian traits.

STYRIA, the south-easterly border-zone of Austria, lies mainly in mountainous country, though it does touch the edges of the Pannonian Basin. Three quite different types of scenery combine to lend Styria a highly individual character.

Upper Styria is 'the land of cow-bells and charcoal-burners, chamois-hunters, iron foundries, scythe-makers and steelworks, of glowing blast-furnaces and mountains red with ore'. The province is girt by the valley of the Enns and the Mur, the latter flowing into the Mürz at Bruck and subsequently turning sharply towards the south. Silver mines were worked at one time in the upper reaches of the Enns valley, and at Schladming up to 1,500 apprentices were employed in the hauling of silver, whilst at Oberhaus both lead and silver were mined until well into the nineteenth century. Today the Erzberg mines are so important as to deserve special mention. The Erzberg, some 6,500 ft high, situated to the south of Eisenerz, contains vast deposits of sparry iron ore; these are extracted in open-cast workings. It is estimated that in the course of more than a thousand years something in excess of 50,000,000 tons have been removed. In another two generations the seams will have been worked out. Ores are

also mined at Donawitz and Leoben. Blast-furnaces, iron and metal foundries, steel- and rolling-mills, all are characteristic features of this 'bronze province'. Bruck on the Mur is an old trading town on the route to the Semmering Pass. In central Styria wide stretches of cultivated land, with fruit-farms and vineyards, have to a great extent replaced the original woodland. Amid this fertile hill-country lies the industrial capital, Graz, which with its population of 227,000, is Austria's second largest city. The various elements incorporated in the community have determined both the character and the growth of this town. Around the cramped and overcrowded old quarter the city walls have been replaced by a series of encircling roads and built-up areas. The outermost of the suburbs are already spilling over into the surrounding countryside. Industry is concentrated in the western part of the town.

Central Styria was in the Tertiary Period a shallow gulf, on whose marshy shores flourished those same forests whose remains are today found as lignite deposits in the area. Köflach and Voitsberg are the best-known centres for this type of mining, and seams more than 120 ft wide have been uncovered. The country east of the Mur is old frontier land, where many castles were built as a protective measure against importunate invaders.

Lower Styria is devoted to farming, and the land has a southerly orientation. Here we find wide areas covered in vineyards, fields of golden maize, flourishing orchards and pleasant woods where beech trees, oaks and Spanish chestnuts add their colour to the gay mosaic of the scenery. Here, too, the Pannonian influence is readily discernible in the low, straw-thatched Slovene houses.

About half of Styria is forest. Certain regions, such as the lower Ennstal, the Mürztal and the country surrounding Mariazell are said to be among the most densely wooded in the world. In such remote corners, the people live and work as they did a hundred years ago, clinging to their own primitive implements and maintaining a way of life that belongs in the past. Some of the customs they observe are centuries old. The Steyr district, where the great curve of the Alps ends, must at one time have undergone basic geological changes; for example, Mürz and the upper Murtal lie in a rift valley. This structural metamorphosis would account for numerous signs of early volcanic activity, for instance, the thermal springs at Gleichenberg, already famous in the Bronze Age.

CARINTHIA. Carinthia, watered by the upper reaches of the Drau, is the perfect example of a completely isolated geographical entity enclosed by mountains. The sunken central basin containing the town of Klagenfurt lies at the heart of the province, guarded by the hills around. Despite its apparent inaccessibility, however, Carinthia is vitally important as a main thoroughfare between the Adriatic and the Vienna Basin. The construction of new roads meant that Klagenfurt gradually became the administrative centre instead of Villach. But as yet Carinthia boasts no really large cities. In the mountainous north-west region most of the towns and villages have developed in the valleys, save where the opening of mines has lured men upward into the barren heights. Gold-mining flourished here in the old days, particularly in the fifteenth and sixteenth centuries, when the daily yield was over 60 lb. Almost no gold is found nowadays. Of much more value are the apparently inexhaustible magnesium deposits at Radenthein, which are extensively worked and produce almost half Austria's magnesium exports. Lignite, also present in abundance, is perhaps Carinthia's most important mineral, and supplies the huge power-house at St Andrä, where one-third of all the electric current is generated. Foremost among the province's natural resources are, however, the forests, covering 44 per cent of the land area. The timber from these forests feeds the saw-mills, cellulose factories and paper-mills. It is also used widely for building purposes, and much of it is exported.

Thirty years ago Carinthia's total population worked on the land. Today the number has fallen to 26 per cent. Nevertheless, her farmers produce enough potatoes, wheat, rye, oats and barley to make her agriculturally the fourth most productive province in the Federation. The principal agricultural areas lie in the hill country and in the flatter regions of Lower Carinthia.

SALZBURG. Until 1803 Salzburg was an ecclesiastical State, later becoming for a short time a secular dukedom. It first formed part of Austria in 1805, passed into the possession of Bavaria between 1810 and 1814, and was finally re-allocated to Austria by the Congress of Vienna—with the exception of the Berchtesgaden area which remained Bavarian by virtue of its rich salt deposits. The province therefore embraces the Salzach valley where it enters Austria, the Lungau and the upper Saalachtal. The countryside is neatly divided up by narrow valleys into what are known as 'Gaus'—a word which simply means a district or province. The Pinzgau, Pongau, Lungau and Tennengau are situated in the mountains, while the Flachgau, flatter than these, as its name suggests, lies in the alpine foreland. Geologically, it was once a part of the lowest basin of the Salzach Glacier (also the origin of the Wallersee and the Trumersee). Here the rich soil has produced lush meadows and fertile farmland, with here and there stretches of bog and moor. The Flachgau is by Austrian standards thickly populated. Salzburg itself, with its splendid situation for trade, was originally a Celtic colony of some note. Today it is for many the world's most attractive city. It boasts a cathedral which has been described as 'the loveliest and most perfect product of late Renaissance architecture on German soil', whilst among its other notable buildings are the Franciscan monastery, the Castle on its rocky eminence, the Mirabell Palace, the house where Mozart was born and a number of beautiful churches. Salzburg attracts more tourist traffic than any other Austrian city, and this has increased steadily since the war. It is expanding rapidly, its population now exceeding 100,000.

The mountain area is naturally more sparsely inhabited. Large tracts of the Lungau and the more recently developed Tennengau are still forest areas, with their sawmills and charcoal burners. The remainder of the province has very little flat countryside, for the wild Salzburg Alps and the Hohe Tauern cover much of the area between them. Nevertheless, this mountain hinterland has its own uses, for it possesses great mineral wealth—copper ore at Mittenberg, magnesium, iron ore, manganese ore and rock salt at Hallein. Furthermore, it harbours famous resorts such as Bad Gastein, Bad Hofgastein and Zell am See. Further features of interest are the huge hydro-electric installation at Kaprun, the Tauern railway and the motor-way over the Grossglockner Pass. As a natural consequence of Salzburg's long history as an ecclesiastical State, the population is devoutly religious. In the remoter corners of the province, the people have to this day retained a most delightful freshness of outlook.

THE TYROL. This old province, whose history dates back 700 years, was split into two as a result of the conditions laid down by the Peace of St Germain, whereby Italy was able to extend her frontiers as far as the Brenner Pass. Some 5,460 sq. miles of land with its 650,000 inhabitants (250,000 of them German) was ceded, and Austria retained only the northern Tyrol; that is to say, the long sweep of the Inn valley from Finzermünz to Kufstein, with its many subsidiary valleys, mostly lying along its right side, the upper Lechtal, excluding the head-water region of the Vorarlberg, and the completely separate eastern Tyrol, accessible only from Salzburg and Carinthia. A series of vital mountain passes lends the Tyrol a special importance, for it occupies an envied position as 'the middle power' between Germany and Italy. The principal pass is the Brenner, cutting straight across the mountain barrier at a height of only 4,500 ft. The construction of the Brenner railway in 1867 greatly increased the value and efficacy of this route.

The Tyrol is a mainly mountainous district, where the most diverse types of rock-strata are welded together. These geological factors not only affect the outward appearance of the different regions, but also radically determine their economy. The mountains of the northern Tyrol are today still heavily wooded, and their rugged contours afford a paradise for mountaineers. In the central zone, the high altitudes of both the cultivated land and the villages and farms is a striking feature. Here barley will grow at 3,600 ft, and on southerly slopes at 6,000 ft, while the sheep graze at altitudes of nearly 10,000 ft. Owing to its height much of the area is barren, and glaciers abound. The Schieferalpen (Slate Alps) are of primary importance in the Tyrol's economy. The soft sub-stratum ensures that the land has gentle contours and fertile soil. Grassy uplands stretch high into the mountains, and above the forests the mountain pastures rise sometimes to the very crests of the ridges. The Tuxer Alps and the Kitzbühel mountains are among the best-known of these regions; the secluded high pastures of the latter constitute one of the most viable regions in the northern Tyrol. The schistous slopes are ideal for ski-ing, so that the Tyrol is the land of mountain railways and ski-lifts. One railway alone, that on the Zugspitze, every year carries 50,000 to 60,000 passengers, thereby earning, like every other branch of the tourist industry, a substantial amount of foreign currency for Austria.

The centres of industry, commerce and civil administration are for the most part located in the valleys: typical examples are the Inn valley—bisected by the sudden narrowing at the Martinswand west of Innsbruck—the Ötztal, Wipptal and Zillertal. They are all glacial formations, with terraced slopes and fertile screes. In these valleys long-established and well-to-do farming communities live and work in close proximity to thriving modern industrial plants, while from the surrounding hills old fortresses and ruined castles look silently down, symbols of the turbulent past.

Innsbruck, despite the loss of the southern Tyrol, has maintained and even improved her status as a commercial centre, for she is now a prosperous town on the frontier with Italy, and the undisputed capital of the province.

Today the Tyrol is at once an industrial and an agricultural region. There has in recent years been a distinct swing away from stock-raising towards alpine dairy-farming. Tyrolean cheeses have already made a name for themselves, and the butter output is steadily mounting. Though a variety of mineral deposits is present in the soil, these are of little significance. On the other hand, much more electric current could be generated, in spite of already existing surpluses.

The introduction of new industries and the increase in trade have combined to oust many of the native customs and traditions. Pagan rites in the guise of Christian festivals do persist here and there, however, in the remoter valleys.

THE VORARLBERG. Let us begin at the Rhine of which this province might be said to be largely an offshoot, for the great river follows the frontier along its whole length, except at Diepoldsau and Lustenau. Here, in the fertile plain warmed by the gentle south wind from Switzerland, we encounter the largest and most productive villages, built either on mountain spurs and hillocks above flood-level, or as bridgeheads on the river itself. The Vorarlberg might easily belong to Switzerland, for not only do they both share an Alemannic ancestry, but strong economic ties also exist between the two neighbours. From the Rhine valley at St Gall the textile industry spread across the river and into the great tributary valleys. Cotton, cellular woollen cloth, silk and artificial silk are produced in bulk, the textile factories employing about half the industrial population. Here and there farming villages have been transformed into textile-producing units, undergoing marked changes in the process. Only some 18 per cent of the working population is now engaged in farming, and the agricultural output would only be sufficient to keep the province going for three months at the outside, despite the high yield of potatoes, maize and oats. In the Montafon, Klostertal and Bregenzerwald areas, as in both the Walser valleys, the population still maintains its original agricultural economy, and in addition a great deal of timber is felled. A striking feature is the preponderance of alpine pasture-land. The area is famous for its dairy produce—above all its cheeses. Despite its small size, the scenery of the Vorarlberg is amazingly varied, sometimes differing appreciably from one valley to another. In the Montafon region pre-Roman place-names are an indication of early colonization: the Walser valleys were first settled and brought under cultivation in the Middle Ages by the migrating Swiss tribe from which the area takes its name. These remote communities tend to live in complete isolation, preserving their ancient ways. Thus, while in the rest of the Vorarlberg all the farm buildings are under one roof, the Walsertäler farmers keep the dwelling-house as a separate unit. The pattern of these agricultural communities changes from one lonely valley to another. Many age-old customs prevail to this day among the settlers of pure Alemannic descent. The advent of Spring is celebrated with fireworks; the villagers take a keen interest in all matters pertaining to birth, sickness and death; and help is automatically given to all those in danger or distress. The wearing of national dress is, however, fast dying out, and only the women of the mountain valleys continue to appear in their traditional costumes, though only on Sundays.

The mineral resources of the region are slight, though many place-names point to large-scale mining in the past, and the bells at Lech are cast in iron mined locally. More important nowadays is the generation of electric power, for as well as consuming much electricity on her own account, the Vorarlberg 'exports' more current than the rest of Austria. Austria's annexation of the Arlberg in 1451 brought that region into increased prominence, and the Vorarlberg gained in stature as a corridor. Her importance would be greatly enhanced by the construction of a canal from the Rhine to Lake Constance, with Bregenz as the terminus, for this would facilitate the importation of large quantities of grain and coal into the eastern alpine region and the reciprocal exportation of iron ore, timber products and building materials.

With this brief description of the provinces of Austria we have sought to bring out the variety of their colourful scenery as well as some of the main differences in their individual economies. It only remains to add a postscript outlining the many variations—great and small—in the land settlement of these zones. It would be impossible to discuss this in any detail. Well-established country villages and modern industrial installations, sports grounds and sedate watering-places, old manor-houses, teeming settlements and tiny hamlets, thick-walled Rhaeto-Romanic villas and spruce, timbered Walser houses—you will find all these the length and breadth of this delightful country. In one district, the dwelling-house and farm buildings will all share a common roof; in another the house stands on its own, away from the animals' quarters. In one valley the little villages may be strung together like a necklace of pearls, and in the next they may have crept far up the sweeping mountain slopes; in mining regions, again, their location is almost entirely determined by the geological sub-stratum.

In contrast to that of the old Danube kingdom, the population of modern Austria is exceedingly close-knit, racially, linguistically and religiously. Out of almost 7,000,000 people, only a small percentage is made up of Croats, Slovenes, Magyars and Czechs. The Roman Catholic religion predominates, and its strength is apparent from the many churches, monasteries, non-secular place-names and religious customs.

No description would be complete without a résumé of the main economic structure of the Second Republic. Only a survey of the country as a whole can reveal her economic strength, a strength which is in the long run the only guarantee of her future progress. 'All things considered, this small State, with its mineral treasures, its natural resources and highly developed industry, is no mean inheritance.' But until 1918 its entire economy depended on the flatter regions around the Danube valley. The loss in that year of vital sources of raw materials, agricultural areas and market outlets, the partial inadequacy of the existing railway system, which had been constructed to fit the requirements of a much larger State, and the uneasy relationship between Vienna and her mountainous hinterland—all these factors demanded radical readjustments and a reassessment of Austria's basic potentialities.

This new orientation appeared at first to be more difficult than had been anticipated. The aftermath of the First World War and the economic decline of the 'thirties engendered a mood of despondency and depression, and often invited the conclusion that the new State should abandon its claims to an independent existence and amalgamate with its German neighbour.

Since the treaty ratification of May 1955 a new Austria has arisen, refreshed and optimistic, and by a combination of her own efforts and assistance from abroad has become an honoured partner in economic affairs. Today her industrial production is two-and-a-half times that of twenty years ago, her national income has grown by more than 50 per cent, and over the same period her unemployment figure has fallen from 33 per cent to 5 per cent. Various factories have contributed to make this economic miracle possible. Agriculture has benefited from a widespread nationalization of techniques and extensive mechanization, the number of tractors, reapers, milking machines and combine-harvesters in service has greatly increased, and consequently production has expanded to such an extent that it is practically sufficient to meet the national consumption.

Thirty-seven per cent of Austria's land area is wooded, and four in every five of these trees are coniferous. Each year timber worth 4 billion Austrian shillings is felled. Equally important is the carpentering industry, which together with the timber trade accounts for a substantial proportion of the country's exports.

The mineral deposits of Austria are considerable, and include lignite, petroleum, iron and manganese ore, magnesium and many other valuable minerals—a wealth which some other countries might well envy. To these must be added the substantial output and reserves of electricity. No other country in central Europe is so well endowed with the means for generating hydro-electric power. Already 10 per cent of this output is channelled to other countries and production could be quadrupled by a relatively small outlay on expansion of generating plant.

Austrian industries are for the most part based on home-produced wood, iron and building materials. Only the textile industry is obliged to import the bulk of its raw material. More than one-third of the industrial production is sold abroad, in consequence of the predominantly agricultural nature of the interior.

Since the Second World War there has been a distinct swing in the regional distribution of the export trade towards the members of OEEC (Organization for European Economic Cooperation). But trade with the U.S.A. has already expanded considerably. The imports of food and coal resulting from the Marshall Aid plan have been absorbed into the normal import programme. If the deliveries in the form of reparations are included, Russia ranks as the third largest importer of Austrian products. The mainly passive balance of trade is achieved above all by the tourist trade whose expansion in the new and revived Austria has exceeded all expectations.

As we have seen, the treaty of St Germain considerably reduced the size of Austria; as a result, her rôle as a political force has probably been played out. She has turned to other tasks. It is on the exploitation of her natural resources and on her own self-awareness that her future will be built—her future not merely as a nationally and economically sound organism, but also as an important link between the peoples of Europe.

NOTES ON THE PLATES

Colour Plates

I SCHÖNBRUNN PALACE: the park. View from one of the two Naiad fountains (by J. B. Hagenauer; end of the eighteenth century) towards the garden front of the main building.

II FORCHTENSTEIN CASTLE in the Rosaliengebirge (Burgenland). See note on Plate 39.

III GRAZ. Clock tower on the southern slopes of the Schlossberg. The symbol of the town, it was completed in 1561.

IV ADMONT MONASTERY: the library. See note on Plate 116.

V VOLDERS, on the Inn. Tower of the church of the former Servite monastery. It repeats the characteristic central plan of the church itself (completed 1654 after plans by Hippolitus Guarinoni). The upper portion of the tower dates from 1730–40.

VI View of RATTENBERG, on the Inn. With its unspoilt appearance this town offers one of the best examples of the architectural style of the Inn region. The façade of the houses is extended beyond the gable ends thus concealing the roof-line, which runs away from the street.

VII The LECHTAL ALPS, near Warth. View towards the Biberkopf (8,530 feet) which marks the German frontier.

Monochrome Pictures

1–25 VIENNA. This city on the Danube was already a settlement in prehistoric times. After the Habsburgs had made it their capital it remained the seat of the Austrian and Holy Roman emperors for five centuries.

1–2 ST STEPHEN'S CATHEDRAL (Stefansdom), originally built as a parish church, was the burial place of the first Austrian dukes. It became an episcopal church in 1469 and a cathedral in 1723. The west front dates from the thirteenth century, the present hall-type church and the south tower, which has become symbolic of the city, were built in the fourteenth and fifteenth centuries. The majestic structure suffered heavy damage in 1945 but this was made good after the war.

2 The pulpit, with carved busts of the four church fathers, was built in 1515 by Anton Pilgram, a native of Brünn in the Upper Rhine district. His self-portrait appears under the steps.

3 High Mass in the CHURCH OF THE CAPUCHINS, founded by Emperor Matthias in 1614 and built 1622–32. A large hospital is connected with the monastery.

4–7 The BELVEDERE, palace of Prince Eugene of Savoy. It comprises two buildings separated by gardens and its noble scale reflects the power wielded by the conqueror of the Turks whose campaigns ushered in a new epoch for south-eastern Europe.

4 This view across the gardens (laid out in 1700) shows the Upper Belvedere, begun in 1721 to designs by Lucas von Hildebrandt.

5 Prince Eugene monument (by A. Fernkorn) in front of the Neue Hofburg. The statue, like the rest of the building, dates from the nineteenth century.

6 Sala terrena in the Upper Belvedere. It leads to the staircase and, with its Atlantid figures, supports the great hall above.

7 Staircase in the Upper Belvedere, a masterpiece of Baroque architecture.

8 The HOFBURG, a complex of buildings which evolved slowly and dates from many different periods. Today its appearance is dominated by the eighteenth-century portions and by the monumental Neue Hofburg (after 1881), designed by Gottfried Semper and Karl Hasenauer and reproduced in this picture.

9-10 The WINTER RIDING SCHOOL, built 1729-35 by J. E. Fischer von Erlach, forms part of the Hofburg. Even today the system of training, carried out with noble Lipizzaner stallions, preserves something of the imperial Habsburg tradition.

11 The HOFBIBLIOTHEK (now the National Library), designed by Fischer von Erlach the Elder and completed by his son in 1735. Our picture shows the domed central hall.

12 The large MUSIKVEREINSSAAL, which has a distinguished musical past, in the Musikvereinsgebäude. This building, constructed 1869-70 by Hansen for the Vienna Music Society, houses a large musicological collection. It is also the headquarters of the Vienna Philharmonic Orchestra and of the famous Universal-Edition.

13 The world-famous VIENNA BOYS' CHOIR (Wiener Sängerknaben) whose history dates back to the court of Emperor Maximilian I.

14-16 The VIENNA STATE OPERA, a centre of operatic tradition which has numbered Gustav Mahler and Richard Strauss among its directors, today retains its musical importance as well as its material splendour. The building, constructed between 1861 and 1869 by Van der Nüll and Siccardsburg, was damaged during the Second World War but has since been restored to its original form.

15 The new auditorium, rebuilt in 1955.

16 A scene from 'Der Rosenkavalier' by Richard Strauss, with libretto by Hugo von Hofmannsthal. The opera, which re-creates the enchanted atmosphere of eighteenth-century Vienna, is one of the composer's best-known works.

17-19 The STADTPARK, laid out in 1863, is also a kind of pantheon. It contains statues of such famous and popular Austrian figures as Johann Strauss (the 'Waltz King'), Makart, Bruckner and Schubert.

20 The BURGTHEATER, like the opera house, is a centre of artistic tradition. Built 1874-80 as the imperial court theatre to plans by Semper and Hasenauer, its history dates back to 1776 and famous first performances held there include the plays of Grillparzer. The theatre was badly damaged during the Second World War but has since been restored.

21 The BUNDESKANZLERAMT (formerly the Privy Court Chancery) at No. 2 Ballhausplatz was built at the beginning of the eighteenth century by Lucas von Hildebrandt. In diplomatic circles 'Ballhausplatz' has much the same significance as 'Quai d'Orsay' or '10 Downing Street'.

22 The KARLSKIRCHE, a centrally planned domed church erected 1716-39 by J. B. Fischer von Erlach and his son for Charles VI. In front of the galleries, linking the central building with the towers, are two great columns, symbols of imperial power.

23 The RINGTURM by night. This tall block near the Augarten bridge houses the Vienna Municipal Insurance. Built in 1953-55 by Erich Boltenstern it breaks into the skyline hitherto dominated by St Stephen's Cathedral.

24-25 After 1792 Beethoven occupied several different residences in Vienna, among them No 8 Mölkerbastel, which he made his home on more than one occasion. The statue in the foreground represents burgomaster Liebenberg, regent of the town during the second Turkish occupation.

25 HEILIGENSTADT, now a suburb of Vienna, where Beethoven also lived. In 1802 he wrote the 'Heiligenstädter Testament'.

26–28 SCHÖNBRUNN PALACE. The palace and gardens (by J. B. Fischer von Erlach) were built outside the gates of Vienna after the end of the seventeenth century when the Turkish peril was over.

26 Lead statue of the Empress Maria Theresa in Hungarian coronation robes (Franz Xaver Messer-schmidt, 1766). The Empress played an important rôle in furthering the architectural progress of Schönbrunn.

27 View of the central building (cf. Colour Plate I).

28 The great gallery, furnished by Maria Theresa, with its allegorical ceiling paintings. The subject represented is 'Austria during the Seven Years' War', the most momentous event of the Empress's reign. The gallery was restored after suffering heavy damage during the Second World War.

29 KLOSTERNEUBURG. View of the monastery and church. The monastery, founded at the beginning of the twelfth century by Leopold III, was closely connected with the ducal residence which was originally here and not in Vienna. The church was adapted to the Baroque during the seventeenth century and the exterior under-went further extensive restoration in the nineteenth. Our picture shows the building by Donato Felice d'Allio (begun 1730), which forms part of a spacious complex intended to resemble the Escorial in design.

30–31 The monastery of HEILIGENKREUZ, in the Vienna Forest (Wienerwald), is the oldest Cistercian abbey in Lower Austria. Founded by Leopold III in 1137, it was built in the twelfth and thirteenth centuries and was extended with new buildings in the seventeenth century.

30 View of the monks' quarters: the 'lower dormitory'.

31 The 'capital hall', which leads to the cloisters, is one of the finest examples of Gothic architecture. It was built in the middle of the thirteenth century.

32 Since 1919 the NEUSIEDLERSEE, with a depth of only 6–10 feet, has marked the boundary with Hungary.

33 RUST, on the shores of the Neusiedlersee, is famous for its vineyards. The low houses, often in a rustic Baroque style, are characteristic of this district which is close to the Hungarian border.

34 The castle of GÜSSING, in the southern part of Burgenland, is one of many fortresses that give this province its name. They were originally built to defend the country against incursions from the east which continued until the seventeenth century. Güssing was once the property of the Batthyany family, who are buried at the foot of the mountain.

35–36 EISENSTADT, the capital of Burgenland, was the resi-dence of the Esterházy princes (5,500 inhabitants).

35 The seventeenth-century residence. Not far distant, just inside the Hungarian border, lies Esterháza, another castle belonging to the Esterházy family. It was here, and later in Eisenstadt, that Haydn spent much of his time as conductor in the household of these music-loving princes (1761–90).

36 The composer's house in the Haydngasse, which now incorporates a commemorative museum.

37–38 Wine-grower's farm and village street in TRAUSDORF, on the Wulka. Both the landscape and the architecture of this region indicate its proximity to Hungary.

39 FORCHTENSTEIN CASTLE, in the Rosaliengebirge. Built by Count Paul von Mattersdorf around 1340, it was used as a fortress during the Turkish invasions of 1529, 1532 and 1683. In 1622 it came into the posses-sion of the Esterházy princes (cf. Colour Plate II).

40 LOCKENHAUS CASTLE, an Esterházy seat near the Hungarian border.

41–42 The castle of RAPOTTENSTEIN, above the River Kamp. Founded by Rapoto von Kuenring in the middle of the twelfth century, the spacious property has buildings dating from the fourteenth and sixteenth centuries.

43–44 The RAXALPE (6,591 feet) and the Vienna Schneeberg (6,808 feet) are among the highest mountains in Lower

Austria. The two, separated by the Höllental, are popular excursion centres for the Viennese.

45-46 SCHÖNGRABERN: sculptures in the apse of the parish church. This important late Romanesque monument (beginning of the thirteenth century), like many other Austrian buildings of the same period, shows a close affinity with the architectural styles of southern Germany.

47-48 ZWETTL was founded in 1137 as a Cistercian monastery by the monks of Heiligenkreuz (Plates 30-31). Its choir, dating from the mid-fourteenth century, is one of the most important architectural monuments of the late Gothic period. The thirteenth-century cloisters are surrounded by the remains of older buildings. The nave of the church, as well as the façade and tower date from the beginning of the eighteenth century.

47 Well-house in the cloisters.

48 View from the south, across the Kamp, with the monastery buildings in the foreground.

49-50 ALTENBURG, a Benedictine monastery founded in 1144, owes its present-day appearance to its seventeenth-century buildings and to the alterations carried out by J. Munggenast in the eighteenth century.

49 The crypt below the library. The walls are decorated with grotesques, among them a 'Dance of Death'.

50 The banqueting-hall wing stands on one of the five courtyards that surround the old monastery church (rebuilt in the eighteenth century).

51-52 GÖTTWEIG was founded as a Benedictine monastery in 1074 by the Bishop of Passau. Like most monasteries it was altered and extended several times before being given its present form by Lucas von Hildebrandt in the eighteenth century.

51 The monastery church stands at the top of a hill, in the centre of the unfinished complex. Its eighteenth-

century façade masks a nave (by Cypriano Biasino) dating from the beginning of the seventeenth century. The choir was built between 1402 and 1431.

52 The magnificent staircase (Kaiserstiege) in the north wing. Built in 1738, it formed part of the extensions by Lucas von Hildebrandt.

53 ST PÖLTEN: interior of the cathedral church. In former times the nucleus of the monastery of St Hippolytus, from whom the town takes its name, the cathedral has since 1785 been the seat of the bishops of western Lower Austria. The twelfth-century structure was rebuilt many times and was finally given its Baroque style at the beginning of the eighteenth century (by J. Prandtauer).

54 The old town of PÖCHLARN, on the Danube, residence of the legendary Margrave Rüdiger who features in the Nibelungenlied. Until 1803 the town formed part of Regensburg.

55 and The DANUBE, near Loiben, at the approach to the
63 Wachau. The river flows through Austria for 219 miles of its total length (1,781 miles). It is navigable all the way and is an important traffic highway, principally serving the ports of Linz and Vienna.

56-57 STEIN-UND-KREMS, originally three separate townships, owes its importance to its salt and wine trades (twelfth century). Fine buildings of the fourteenth and fifteenth centuries have given the town its characteristic appearance.

56 View across the battlemented PASSAUERHOF towards the Frauenbergkirche (fourteenth century) and the parish church of St Nikolaus (fifteenth century).

57 Renaissance portal of the former imperial customs house (Mauthaus) on the Steiner Landstrasse.

58 The DANUBE near Stein, looking west.

59-60 The parish church (originally part of an Augustinian monastery) at DÜRNSTEIN in the Wachau. The building, by J. Munggenast (1721–25), is a fine example of Baroque architecture.

59 The church seen from the north. In front are the monastery buildings with a fine portal.

60 The castle above the town, built in the middle of the twelfth century by Joh. von den Kuenringern (cf. 41–42). Richard Cœur de Lion was a prisoner here in 1190.

61 and WEISSENKIRCHEN, one of the largest townships in
65 the Wachau. In 1531 the fifteenth-century parish church was fortified against the Turks and surrounded with a wall.

65 The Teisenhofer-Hof, built in 1542, formed part of the fortifications.

62 The ancient town of ST MICHAEL, on the left bank of the Danube. Like Weissenkirchen it has a fortified church, built 1500–23.

64 and WINE HARVEST in the Wachau district. Weissen-
66 kirchen appears in the background of plate 64.

67 MAUER, NEAR MELK. Detail from the High Altar of the parish church, for long a place of pilgrimage. The carving of the Madonna in Glory on the altar is one of the most important sculptures of its period (c. 1520). It is by an unknown artist whose work can also be traced in Vienna.

68 MARIA-LAACH, at the foot of the Jauerling. The altar to the Virgin Mary is an exceptionally well-preserved and hence rare example of early fifteenth-century carving at its most graceful.

69 PERSENBEUG CASTLE, on the Danube, mentioned in documents as early as the tenth century. The present complex dates from the beginning of the seventeenth century (1617–21).

70 SCHALLABURG CASTLE, near Melk, originally a medieval structure rebuilt 1572–1600 by Wilhelm von

Losenstein. The arcaded courtyard, a feature derived from Italian architecture, is characteristic of castles dating from this period and is especially well represented in Austria.

71 SCHÖNBÜHEL CASTLE, on the Danube (also shown in colour on the wrapper). Originally held in fee from the diocese of Passau, it later passed to the counts of Starhemberg who founded a Servite monastery there in 1666. The castle, which is impressively situated at the entrance to the Wachau, was given its present form as late as the beginning of the nineteenth century.

72–74 The Benedictine monastery of MELK, whose prominent position on a spur of the Dunkelsteiner Forest reveals its past as a medieval fortress. Melk originated in the eleventh century, later became a fortified monastery and, under Abbot Berthold Dietmayer at the beginning of the eighteenth century, was developed into the present magnificent complex by the Tyrolese architect Jakob Prandtauer.

72 View across the Danube towards the monastery and church.

73 The dome above the transept of the church, built 1702–26 and restored 1949–50 after a fire. Some of the most famous artists of their day contributed to the decorations (among them, Paul Troger, Antonio Bibbiena, J. M. Rottmayr).

74 View from the library which, as in all Benedictine monasteries, is a centre of learning and culture. The figures by the door, representing two of the four faculties, are by J. Pöbl.

75–76 SEITENSTETTEN, a Benedictine monastery founded in 1112. The church was built between 1254 and 1300 while the monastery buildings date from the seventeenth and eighteenth centuries.

75 The magnificent main staircase in the north wing of the monastery, with banisters by Joh. Adam Kühn (1746).

76 The façade of the church, rebuilt in the Baroque manner by J. Prandtauer (1701–11). It stands at the centre of the spacious complex whose design was based on that of the Escorial.

77–79 ST FLORIAN, an Augustine monastery for prebendaries, is one of the most famous of all monastic foundations. The medieval buildings were altered and enlarged after the end of the seventeenth century; Carlo Antonio Carlone (after 1686) was responsible for the church, Jakob Prandtauer and his successors for the extensive monastery buildings.

77 The famous open staircase, based on plans by Prandtauer.

78 The magnificent organ (1770–83, by F. X. Krismann), known as the Bruckner organ. Bruckner, teacher and organist at St Florian from 1845 until 1856, lies buried in the church.

79 View of the monastery and church.

80 High Altar of the late Gothic parish church at KEFERMARKT, with SS Peter, Wolfgang and Christopher. The altar was founded at the end of the fifteenth century but its present composition differs from the original one. So far the artistic authorship of the altar remains unknown.

81–82 LINZ, industrial town and cathedral city, is the capital of Upper Austria (c. 200,000 inhabitants).

81 The bridge across the Danube (820 feet wide) leads to the Hauptplatz (main square), which is the focal point of the city. To the left stands the old cathedral where Bruckner was organist from 1856 to 1868. Farther to the left can be seen the steeple of the town church. To the extreme right of the picture can be seen a wing of the castle, built c. 1600.

82 The UNITED AUSTRIAN IRON AND STEEL WORKS (Vereinigte Österreichische Eisen- und Stahlwerke, also known as VOEST, account for the greater part of the country's iron and steel production (67% of the total output of pig-iron, 40% of the total output of steel in 1956). The iron ore is mined in Styria.

83–85 STEYR, on the Enns, with its ancient castle, has since the twelfth century developed into a prosperous town which owes its wealth mainly to its iron industry. (The iron from the Erzberg is carried down the river Enns.)

83 The Stadtplatz (town square) with the Rathaus (town hall) and the Dominican church. The former (centre of picture), built 1765–71 by J. G. Hayberger (a native of Steyr), is one of the finest examples of Austrian rococo.

84 Confluence of the Steyr and the Enns. On the bank stand the fourteenth-century hospital and the church of St Michael, built 1631–72.

85 The Schnallentor in the Steyrdorf quarter (1613) with its restored sgraffito decorations. This decorative technique (German 'Putzschnitt' or 'Kratzputz') is commonly found on the walls of Steyr houses.

86–88 KREMSMÜNSTER, save St Peter's in Salzburg, is the oldest monastic foundation in Austria. The abbey was founded in 777 by Duke Tassilo of Bavaria but owes its present form to changes and additions carried out around 1700.

86 Founder's tomb from the beginning of the fourteenth century.

87 The Tassilo chalice in the sacristy, a priceless relic of the eighth century. The base bears the inscription: TASSILO DUX FORTIS LIUTPIRC VIRGO REGALIS.

88 The monastic fish ponds: five basins surrounded by arcaded walks, dating from 1691.

89–90 The lake castle of ORT, near Gmunden, which stands on an island in the Traunsee, is linked by a bridge with the castle on the mainland. The present buildings date mainly from the sixteenth century, although the foundation is of medieval origin.

91–92 HALLSTATT, on the Hallstättersee.

92 Corpus Christi procession. This is held in boats on the lake, a custom that also prevails in Traunkirchen.

93 TRAUNKIRCHEN, on the Traunsee. The pulpit (erected 1753) in the parish church, with its representation of the Miracle of the Fishes, an allusion also to the principal occupation of the town's inhabitants. An abbey stood on this site even before 900. Until 1773 the church belonged to the Jesuits, which accounts for the portrait of St Francis Xavier on the tester.

94 BRAUNAU, on the Inn. The old border town with its parish church, seen from the Bavarian bank.

95 HALLEIN, on the Salzach, has one of the oldest salt mines in the province of Salzburg, which takes its name from this commodity.

96 VORDERER GOSAUSEE (3,061 feet), with a view of the Dachstein (9,829 feet).

97 LOFER, in the Pinzgau district, not far from the Berchtesgaden country.

98 ST GILGEN, at the northernmost point of the Wolfgangsee. Mozart's mother, Anna Maria Pertl, was born here in 1720 and his sister 'Nannerl' made the town her home after 1784.

99–100 ST WOLFGANG. View south towards the Sparber (4,918 feet).

100 The Coronation of the Virgin, Michael Pacher's masterpiece on the High Altar of the parish church (1471–80). Pacher was probably born in Brixen (Bressanone) and is thought to have died in Salzburg.

101–11 SALZBURG developed from a Roman settlement and has retained its importance through the ages. Today the town centre, which has remained almost completely unspoilt, is largely composed of seventeenth-century episcopal buildings and dwelling-houses dating mainly from the eighteenth century. The city is uniquely situated in the shadow of the fortress (the greater part of which was built by Archbishop Leopold von Keutschach at the beginning of the sixteenth century) and in general layout and appearance owes much to the planning of Archbishop Wolf Dietrich von Raitenau (1587–1612). Indeed, in their rôle as lords of the province the archbishops generally left their mark on the town. For many years music, especially the music of Mozart, has played an important rôle in the life of the city while the now world-famous Festival, initiated in 1920 by Max Reinhardt, Hugo von Hofmannsthal and Richard Strauss, has added new glory to the name of Salzburg.

101 View from the right bank of the Salzach across the cathedral to the fortress of Hohensalzburg. On the right can be seen the Residenz and the steeple of the Franciscan church.

102 The gardens of the Mirabell Palace. The fortress in the background was intentionally brought into the design.

103 The Kollegienkirche in the centre of the town. This university church, built 1694–1707, is one of the chief works of J. B. Fischer von Erlach and is a striking example of Baroque architecture.

104 The Mirabell Palace. Part of Lucas von Hildebrandt's superb staircase with putti by G. R. Donner.

105 The cathedral, built 1614–28 by Santino Solari. Legend has it that the archbishop set fire to the old building in order to make room for its successor, which represented a novel architectural design for north of the Alps. The marble-clad façade forms one end of the square and has for many years provided a setting for Festival performances of Hofmannsthal's 'Everyman', originally directed by Max Reinhardt.

Mozart's sacred compositions were given their first performances in this church.

106 Salzburg Festival: theatrical rehearsal in the Felsenreitschule, which once formed part of the archiepiscopal stables (Hofmarstall). The arcades were hewn out of the rock of the Mönchsberg (1693).

107 The cemetery near the Romanesque church of St Peter, where Michael Haydn (d. 1806) and Mozart's sister are buried.

108 Mozart's birthplace at No. 9 Getreidegasse (our picture shows the back of the house), which now contains the Mozart Museum. Apart from its historical significance, the building is also a good example of urban architecture in the Inn and Salzach regions. The tall façade conceals the true roof-line of the house (cf. Colour Plate VI).

109 Corridor above the archway which links the cathedral with the Residenz and adjoining buildings. They were built by G. A. Dario between 1658 and 1663. The plaster-work on the ceiling exemplifies the rich and heavy ornamentation of the period.

110 The horse-trough near the Hofmarstall, an impressive and elaborate installation which almost conceals its original utilitarian function. The sculpture of the horse-tamer is by M. B. Mandl (1695). Immediately behind are the steep cliffs of the Mönchsberg.

111 The pleasure-palace of Hellbrunn near Salzburg, villa suburbana of the archbishops, was built between 1613 and 1619 by Santino Solari, architect of the cathedral.

112 BAD GASTEIN (3,510 feet), famous spa whose warm springs ($82\frac{1}{2}$–$116\frac{1}{2}$°F.) have attracted—and still attract—visitors of title and wealth from all over the world. The town, with its characteristic hotel buildings and pump rooms, is divided by the cascading waters of the Ache. Our picture shows the bridge between the Kurkasino and the Straubinger Platz.

113 'SCHÖNPERCHTEN' in the Pongau district. The masked carnival lasts from Martinmas until Ash Wednesday and reaches its climax on the night of January 5th–6th. The enormously tall headdresses weigh up to 90 lb. The custom is nearly a thousand years old.

114 The ZELLERSEE, in the Pinzgau district (2,461 feet).

115 The REICHENSTEIN (7,372 feet), in the Ennstaler Alps, near Admont.

116 ADMONT. The library of the Benedictine monastery (see also Colour Plate IV). Founded by the diocese of Salzburg in 1074, it is, like Gottweig and others, one of the 'colonial' monasteries which after the twelfth century came under the patronage of the dukes of Austria. In 1865 a fire destroyed the church and a large part of the monastery buildings. The library (completed 1776), with its mural paintings by Bartolomeo Altomonte and sculptures by J. Th. Stammel, testifies to the former splendour of the establishment.

117–18 The ERZBERG (Iron Mountain) in Styria is, with the Hüttenberg in Carinthia, Austria's richest source of iron ore. Here, at the largest iron mine in Europe, three-quarters of the country's total output is produced (Austria's total output in 1956 approached $3\frac{1}{4}$ million tons). The basic iron content of the ore is relatively low (32%), but its purity and manganese content make mining here a worthwhile undertaking and one that plays an important part in Austria's national economy. The mine, together with the other basic industries, was nationalized in 1948.

119 LEOPOLDSTEINERSEE, near Eisenerz (2,133 feet).

120 SECKAU ABBEY was founded as a monastery for prebendaries in 1140. Its twelfth-century church is one of the outstanding monuments of Romanesque architecture and, unlike most other churches belonging to the large monasteries, was not refashioned in the Baroque style. It contains the mausoleum (end of the sixteenth century) of Archduke Karl von Steiermark.

In front of the entrance are two early Gothic lions, one of which is reproduced in our photograph.

121-22 BRUCK-AN-DER-MUR. The town was planned and laid out between the Mur and the Mürz by King Ottokar Przemysl, after having been both a Roman and an early medieval settlement.

121 The CORN-MEASURER'S HOUSE, built 1499–1505 for Pangraz Kornmesser. With its arcades and loggia it clearly shows the influence of Venetian architecture.

122 So-called wrought-iron well in the Hauptplatz (main square). With the exception of the wheel, which is modern, this dates from 1626.

123 The castle of SCHLAINING in the southern part of Burgenland was built in the thirteenth century and, like almost all defensive constructions in this part of the country, originally formed part of a Hungarian fortress against the West. After its capture by Austria in 1529 it was incorporated into the chain of defences against the Turks.

124 MARIAZELL, founded about the middle of the thirteenth century and made part of the monastic foundation of St Lambrecht, is one of the chief pilgrimage churches in Austria. The hall church built by Louis of Hungary at the end of the fourteenth century was enlarged and adapted to the Baroque style by Domenico Sciassia, the monastery's chief architect, between 1644 and 1683. Various Italian masters were responsible for the magnificent stucco decorations. View down the nave towards the Gnadenkapelle and High Altar (J. B. Fischer von Erlach).

125 The RIEGERSBURG, situated on a steep basalt crag, was mentioned in the twelfth century as the residence of the Wildonier family. The inner court, with its fine arcades, dates from the seventeenth century.

126,127 GRAZ, the capital of Styria, is also the second
and 129 largest town in Austria (227,000 inhabitants). Of

historical importance since the end of the twelfth century, it was besieged by the Turks in 1478 and 1480 and made into a fortress in the sixteenth century. In 1527 the town accepted the Reformation but this was revoked by Archduke Ferdinand in 1590.

126 The Landeszeughaus contains a unique collection of armour intended for the Styrian mercenaries who were called out in times of crisis. Our picture shows equestrian armour from the sixteenth century.

127 The Hauptplatz (main square) with a view of the Schlossberg and clock tower (cf. Colour Plate III). In the centre stands the memorial fountain to Archduke John (d. 1859).

129 Arcaded court of the Landhaus, a complex built between the sixteenth and nineteenth centuries. The main building, which includes the fine courtyard, was completed between 1557 and 1565 to designs by Domenico dell'Allio. It is one of the many examples of North Italian architecture in Austria.

128 The monastery of ST LAMBRECHT. View of the church and buildings of the famous Benedictine monastery, founded in the eleventh century. In front of the nave, to the left, stands the charnel-house, a circular structure of the twelfth century. The monastery buildings by Domenico Sciassia were begun in 1639 (cf. Plate 124).

130 Until 1803 FRIESACH was the property of the archbishops of Salzburg, who built the fortified castle above the town (dating back to the twelfth century). The town is still encircled by its medieval wall. Our view shows the Hauptplatz (main square) with the Stadtbrunnen (town fountain) of 1563.

131 ST VEIT-AN-DER-GLAN was the property of the bishops of Bamberg until 1173. Later it became the residence of the dukes of Carinthia and remained the capital of the province until 1518. The Rathaus (town hall) in the main square has a splendid Baroque façade dating from 1754. Above the portal, originally of late Gothic origin,

is a cast metal relief with an excerpt from the old Saxon law code (1468).

132-33 HOCHOSTERWITZ belonged to Salzburg from 860 until the twelfth century. Later it passed, first to the dukes of Carinthia and, in 1541, to the Khevenhüller barons who gave the castle its present impressive form (second half of the sixteenth century).

132 View of the castle rock from the north-west. The ascent, lined by a wall penetrated by a series of towered gateways, spirals up the rock on which the castle is perched.

133 View of the surrounding countryside from the castle.

134 View of NEUDENSTEIN CASTLE (built 1329), on the left bank of the Drau, with the Hochobir (7,020 feet) in the Karawanken range.

135 MARIA WÖRTH, a small peninsula in the Wörthersee which was once the property of the Bishop of Freising. Our picture shows the parish church (formerly the provost's church) whose basic structure dates from the middle of the twelfth century, when the church was founded. On the right stands the thirteenth-century charnel-house.

136 The HOCHOBIR: view from Griffen across the Jauntal. Griffen Castle, originally built by the bishops of Bamberg, has long been a ruin.

137 KLAGENFURT. Armorial Hall in the Landhaus, with murals by Jos. Ferd. Fromiller and the coats of arms of the Carinthian diet, who owned the town until the middle of the nineteenth century. Founded in 1224 at the junction of important trade highways, the town became the capital of Carinthia only in 1518 (cf. Plate 131). Today it has 63,000 inhabitants.

138 The ROSENTAL (Rose Valley), at the foot of the Karawanken range, running along the border between Austria and Yugoslavia.

139 BAYERHOFEN CASTLE, at Wolfsberg, a building with a fine arcaded courtyard dating from the middle of the sixteenth century.

140 The little town of STRASSBURG, in the Gurktal, nestling below the castle of the prince-bishops of Gurk, was mentioned in documents as early as the end of the twelfth century. The parish church was once part of a collegiate monastery.

141-43 GURK CATHEDRAL was founded in 1072 and was, until 1787, the centre of a large diocese whose members held the rank of princes. The cathedral church, a remarkably well-preserved structure dating from the end of the twelfth century, rises above a crypt (Plate 142) whose vaults are supported by a hundred white marble pillars. The frescoes above the western gallery date from the early thirteenth century and depict a Christological cycle. Plate 143 shows a detail from the story of the Creation.

144 SPITTAL-AN-DER-DRAU: arcaded courtyard in the palace of the Porcia princes, built in the sixteenth century by an unknown Italian architect for Gabriel Salamanca, Count of Ortenburg.

145 HEILIGENBLUT (4,196 feet), at the foot of the Gross-glockner. The St Christopher fresco (c. 1500) on the parish church seen through the courtyard gate. The phial of Sacred Blood which gave the place its name is preserved in this church.

146-49 The GROSSGLOCKNER, Austria's highest mountain (12,460 feet).

146 Looking towards the peak of the Grossglockner and the base of the Pasterze, the longest glacier in the eastern Alps ($6\frac{1}{4}$ miles).

147 The Archduke Johann Hut (11,368 feet), on the way to the summit of the Grossglockner.

148-49 On the Grossglockner pass road which runs from Bruck an der Salzach, via Heiligenblut to Lienz.

The so-called Glacier road branches off halfway and offers magnificent views of the Grossglockner and its glacier.

150 TAUERN POWER STATION AT KAPRUN. View of the Limberg dam with its 394-foot wall. This dams the Ache and takes its waters through a sluice gate to the power station. With four other dams it forms part of a vast and intricate system which uses melted snow from the mountains to produce hydro-electric power, supplying 825 million kilowatt-hours a year. The plants have all been built since 1946.

151 KUFSTEIN CASTLE, with the Kaiserturm, was once the property of the bishops of Regensburg after which it was held in fee by the Bavarian dukes. It went over to the Tyrol in 1504. The fortress was abandoned in 1882.

152 MÜNICHAU CASTLE, near Reith, with the Kaiser-gebirge in the background. The castle, residence of the family of the same name, was built about the middle of the fifteenth century. Our view, from the south, shows the keep and the dwelling quarters.

153 KITZBÜHEL, district capital and a well-known winter sport resort. The two adjacent churches are the parish church (on the left) and the Frauenkirche.

154 The 'WILDE KAISER', a mountain massif made up of belemnite-marls, east of Kufstein.

155 The INN VALLEY, near Wiesing, at the mouth of the Achental and the Zillertal (in the background).

156 SCHWAZ, in the Inn Valley. The impressive parish church, built 1489-1534, bears witness to the prosperity brought to the town by silver mining around 1500. Below the altars, now no longer in existence, there is once supposed to have been a work by Veit Stoss.

157-59 The ZILLERTAL, well-known winter and summer resort, is probably the most famous of the tributary valleys of the Inn Valley. Its many ramifications run right up to the ridge of the Ziller Alps which now form the frontier with Italy.

157 and 159 Two chapels near Finkenberg, where the Tuxertal and several other valleys run into the Zillertal.

158 Typical wooden farmhouse at Gerlos (Gerlostal).

160 and The ancient town of SOLBAD HALL, in the Inn 163 Valley was, like many places of the same or similar name, founded in conjunction with a salt mine. It has been a town since 1303. The dwelling-houses in the narrow old streets have kept their well-preserved fifteenth- and sixteenth-century exteriors. The Inn Valley, which is both deep and wide (1,844 feet at this point) affords an impressive and unimpeded view of the mountains (cf. Plate 164).

161-62 OLD INN SIGNS at:

161 Tarrenz in the Gurgltal.

162 Schwaz.

164-68 INNSBRUCK, capital of the province of the Tyrol with 95,000 inhabitants, lies on the main Brenner route. As a town it was relatively insignificant until the fifteenth century when the dukes of Tyrol and later the Emperors Maximilian I and Ferdinand I made it their seat. From that time until well into the eighteenth century the court left its imprint on the town. Fine patrician houses and splendid court residences bear witness to Innsbruck's great past; its strategic position on an important rail and road thoroughfare ensures for it an equally vital rôle at the present day.

164 Maria-Theresien-Strasse with the Annasäule (1706) and, in the background, the impressive north wall of the Inn Valley.

165 The 'Goldene Dachl', was built c. 1500 for the Emperor Maximilian I. It covers the spectators' balcony from which members of the court used to

watch the games, and is decorated with reliefs (probably by Niklas Türing) and murals (by Jorg Kölderer). The building takes its name from the copper-gilt tiles on the roof.

166 The Helbling Haus with its superb rococo façade (by Anton Gigl, c. 1730). This conceals a late medieval structure.

167–68 Memorial tomb of the Emperor Maximilian I in the Hofkirche. The church was built between 1553 and 1563 to house the monument, which was never completed. In its present form it comprises the sarcophagus and twenty-eight over-life-size bronze figures (1508–50) of the Emperor's ancestors, modelled by different artists and cast by Gilg Sesselschreiber and other craftsmen, including the Nuremberg master P. Vischer (statue of Artus).

167 Statue of King Artus, after a design by Dürer.

168 Statues of (from left to right): Clovis, Philip the Fair, Rudolf of Habsburg, Albert the Wise.

169 KALVARIENBERG (Calvary hill) at ARZL, not far from Innsbruck. The chapel was built in 1666 and restored in 1777.

170 PESTKAPELLE (Plague Chapel) near Schattwald in the upper Vilstal.

171 Along the FERN PASS, between Nassereith and Ehrwald.

172 The ZUGSPITZE (9,721 feet), above Ehrwald. It forms the corner-buttress of the Wetterstein mountains, and a part of the frontier with Germany.

173 GASTHOF 'STERN' at Ötz, a characteristic farmhouse of the upper Inn Valley, with murals dating from 1573 and 1615.

174 On the SEELENFERNER slopes below the Hintere Seelenkogel (11,391 feet) in the Gurgltal, Ötztal Alps.

175–76 'SCHEMENLAUFEN', a carnival (Fasching) custom, at Imst. The procession is accompanied by witches and other grotesque masked figures.

177 BRIDGE ACROSS THE INN, near Roppen.

178 NAUDERSBERG CASTLE, owned by the provincial rulers after 1300, is situated in the upper Inn Valley, near the border with the Lower Engadine.

179 Scenery near IMST, at the junction of the Gurgltal and the Inn Valley.

180 VALLUGA (9,222 feet), near St Anton, on the border between the Tyrol and the Vorarlberg. A cable railway (built 1953–54) runs to the mountain-top.

181–3 COURTING DANCES. The traditional dances, once associated particularly with the Austrian Alps (but also practised elsewhere) have still in part survived.

181 The famous SCHUHPLATTLER, a Bavarian-Tyrolean dance for men.

182 The RANGLER, another dance for men but, in contrast with the Schuhplattler, a stylized tussle.

183 BALZTANZ, a courting dance in which both men and girls take part.

184 View of LECH (4,747 feet), principal locality of the Tannberg area. Lech was founded by emigrants from the Valais in Switzerland, who played a prominent part in developing the Vorarlberg and left their stamp on the architecture and place-names of the region (e.g. Walsertal).

185 Chair-lift on the SEEKOPF, in the Lechtaler Alps.

186 The VALLUGAGRAT (8,694 feet). These heights can be reached by a cable railway (cf. Plate 180).

187–9 Skiing on the ARLBERG. Plate 188 shows the Zürsersee descent.

190-1 The MONTAFON. View across the valley towards the Mittagspitze (7,116 feet). All the rivers in this region flow either into the Rhine or into Lake Constance.

192 FELDKIRCH, with a population of 15,000, is situated at the junction of the Ill and the upper Rhine Valley. It is the commercial centre of the Vorarlberg (textile industry). Its pleasant situation below the Schattenburg and its well-preserved arcaded houses give this town at the country's western approach the welcoming and attractive appearance still retained by most Austrian towns. Our view is along the Marktgasse to the Johanneskirche.

193 Costume from the BREGENZERWALD (Bregenz Forest). The costumes, like the region and its inhabitants, have German affinities.

194 BREGENZ, capital of the Vorarlberg. View across Lake Constance into the upper Rhine Valley, which divides Switzerland and Austria. The mountains in the background are the foot of the Rätikon (left) and the Säntis massif.

PHOTOGRAPHIC SOURCES

Most of the photographs were taken by Toni Schneiders of Lindau specially for this book. They have been supplemented as under:

Dr Benesch, 146
Franz Hausmann, Vienna, 16
Dr M. Hürlimann, 8, 11, 17, 18, 20, 21, 24, 94, 95, 107, 108, 162, 166
Kopetzky, 9, 10

Photo Nussbaumer, 177
Österreichische Fremdenverkehrswerbung, 19, 27, 82
Österreichische Montangesellschaft, 117
Lothar Rübelt, Vienna, 3, 12, 13, 14, 15, 23, 106, 113, 134, 141, 148, 173, 181, 182, 183, 185, 186, 187
Helga Schmidt-Glassner, 1
Dr Straberger, 147
Tauernkraftwerk AG Kaprun, 150

INDEX OF PLACE-NAMES